Advance Praise for
Raising Your Organization's Largest Gifts

"Raising the gifts required for achievement of an organization's most ambitious goals requires board members and senior administrative leaders to understand how principal gift fundraising differs from other fundraising efforts and to have a shared understanding of how to build a culture that inspires these gifts. As a CEO, I have experienced first-hand the wisdom of Ron's advice, and I'm excited about the impact his book will have on organizations throughout the country. I recommend it to every board member, chief executive, chief development officer, and other leader charged with raising an organization's largest and most transformational gifts."
  —**Jena Hausmann,** President and CEO,
    Children's Hospital Colorado

"Ron Schiller has written a book that is a highly polished jewel. Ron leads you by the hand, step-by-step through all the elements in identifying and securing principal gifts. There's an immensely helpful reminder about the importance of the key 40 top-of-mind potential donors. What I liked best was the section on the uniqueness of donors. Each requires a special strategy. The book is extremely well written— there isn't a wasted word. You will love the book and find it extremely helpful."
  —**Jerold Panas,** author, *Mega Gifts*

"Today's chief development officers are being called upon to raise larger and more impactful gifts to advance their institutions' top priorities and aspirations. Schiller's book reminds us that principal gift fundraising is not the same as major gift fundraising. This important resource encourages us to think and act differently to ensure the success of our work."
  —**Kevin Heaney,** Vice President for Advancement,
    Princeton University

"Once again, Ron Schiller has provided an invaluable service to advancement professionals and volunteer and organizational leaders. Much as in his previous works *Belief and Confidence* and *The Chief Development Officer*, Ron deftly explores one of the most critical topics in fundraising in ways that make it seem far less daunting. How can colleges and universities of any size keep pace when successful fundraising today depends upon a handful of the most significant and transformational gifts? Ron helps answer the question in practical ways that address organizational culture and mindset. It's not a matter of clever tricks and smooth salesmanship, but one of meaningful, authentic relationships with your most dedicated partners. For institutions that might fret about what a "90/10" or "98/2" fundraising paradigm might portend for them, this book is just the guide they need."

—**Sue Cunningham,** President & CEO, Council for
Advancement and Support of Education

"This is a great resource for all of us responsible for building relationships with our institutions' key philanthropic partners. Ron reminds us about the importance of keeping those donors at the top of our mind as we go about the regular business of the university, and that big gifts are almost always inspired by big ideas. Ron's advice on building a joyful career in advancement is a welcome read to those of us engaged in this noble profession."

—**Scott Mory,** Vice President for University Advancement,
Carnegie Mellon University

Raising Your Organization's Largest Gifts

Raising Your Organization's Largest Gifts

A PRINCIPAL GIFTS HANDBOOK

Ronald J. Schiller

COUNCIL FOR ADVANCEMENT
AND SUPPORT OF EDUCATION®

London • Mexico City • Singapore • Washington, DC

Cover design: Kris Apodaca
Cover image credit: munandme/iStock/Getty Images Plus

London · Mexico City · Singapore · Washington, DC

Advancing education to transform lives and society.

www.case.org

CONTENTS

FOREWORD

Like most of my favorite books, this one brings clarity to a topic I've been ruminating about lately: How should we be doing principal gifts development in an age when there seem to be so many more generous givers, giving such inspiring gifts? In *Raising Your Organization's Largest Gifts: A Principal Gifts Handbook*, Ron Schiller provides a framework.

I was fortunate to learn most of what I consider important in development from David R. Dunlop, who directed the major and principal gift programs at Cornell University for more than 35 years. Dave also wrote and taught on the subject of highly personalized fundraising and philanthropic motivation and was one of the first development leaders—along with individuals at institutions like Stanford, Harvard and Massachusetts Institute of Technology—to recommend that we needed to have a different development approach for a few of our most generous donors. Based on that idea, Dave established the first principal gifts program at Cornell, and Ron and I had the pleasure of working with him.

The ideas that created the rationale for highly personalized fundraising were both profoundly new but also obvious reflections of how a few donors and volunteers thought about their organizations. Dave described it as the need for a different "posture" toward individuals who had come to think of the university as their highest philanthropic priority. This new posture extended into all the ways we invited these close friends to engage with the university with an emphasis on building close and trusting relationships, the type of relationships that Ron accurately refers to as philanthropic "partnerships." When Dave recommended to Cornell's leadership that a small group of friends be considered for this new approach, he identified just 22 couples and individuals.

Nearly 30 years later, that focus seems impossible given the number of wealthy prospective donors we are in a position to know. Information technology puts us in easy reach of so many people who could make a positive difference with their giving. At the same time as we've seen the narrowing of top gifts move from 80 percent of dollars coming from 20 percent of donors to 98 percent of dollars coming from 2 percent of donors, we've also seen the population of generous and capable prospective donors grow significantly. In fact, it sometimes seems like there are many more generous givers than ideas inspiring enough to compel them. Principal gift programs have expanded in order to respond to this reality. At some organizations, the list of donors and prospective donors includes 200 to 300 couples and individuals. Yet, even with so many high-potential donors, a more focused approach is still possible and important.

A key consideration of *Raising Your Organization's Largest Gifts: A Principal Gifts Handbook* is the role of identification and focus in realizing transforming gifts. Ron directs us to the top 10 to 12 largest gifts at any organization and thinks about the characteristics of the donors who give them. In that process, he points back to the observation Dave and Cornell University made in 1989: There are substantial differences between prospective donors—even very wealthy ones—and generous friends who have the potential to be among the organization's top philanthropic partners.

Ron and I teach a conference for the Council for Advancement and Support of Education on this subject. "Inspiring the Largest Gifts of a Lifetime" was created by Dave and Robert Sharpe, who has written the essay in this book describing ultimate gifts. Dave and Robert thought there needed to be a forum for exploring this different way of thinking about donors of our largest gifts. Every year we meet development professionals from organizations around the world, many of whom are either starting a new program in highly individualized fundraising, or seeking to strengthen the one they have. One of the things we have noticed is the pressure many of them feel to operate these programs just like major and campaign fundraising programs with the same timelines and expectations but with the hope of receiving gifts with many more zeroes.

With this book, Ron turns our attention and our programs back in the right direction. While acknowledging that we do seem to have more generous prospective donors to engage and ask for support, he reminds us that our largest, extraordinarily generous gifts are given by only a few and their relationships to our organizations are of an entirely different flavor. Relying on the things he has learned from the philanthropists with whom he has worked in the past, and whose observations are the heart of his earlier book, *Belief and Confidence*, Ron unpacks the characteristics of these individuals and the programs that are prepared to work with them.

Looking at the ideas of culture, leadership, shared objectives, big ideas, relationship building, engagement and stewardship, Ron suggests practices that optimize our work with these special friends. Since "largest" gifts vary both for the organization and the donor, the ideas in this book transcend differences of scale and apply to organizations of many types and all sizes.

Ron rightfully points out that an organization's largest gifts have an outsized influence on the overall degree of its fundraising reach and success, and that the first donor to step up to an organization's largest gift, no matter what size, creates the possibility of other generous gifts. He also notes that they can move an organization in an entirely new direction, making it critically important that the largest gifts spring from a close and trusting partnership with the organization's leader.

I started this piece writing about Dave Dunlop at Cornell University and how his thinking influenced this field and many of the ideas in this book. One of the characteristics Ron and Dave share is the joy they find in philanthropy and with the people who do development work. That joy runs through this book, especially in the stories Ron uses to illustrate his points, and it's the better for it.

Read *Raising Your Organization's Largest Gifts: A Principal Gifts Handbook* to be reminded of the ideas upon which this practice is based, to help shape a new principal gift program, or to refocus your organization's efforts with its most generous donors, and most of all, as Ron recommends, to inspire your "joyful career in philanthropy."

Rebecca Tseng Smith
Senior Executive Director of Development,
University of California San Diego

INTRODUCTION

For most organizations, the giving decisions of a small number of philanthropic partners determine the organization's overall *scale* of accomplishment and extent of mission fulfillment. Framed another way, most organizations find that a very small number of donors provide the largest and most impactful philanthropic gifts. Accordingly, this book argues that while organizational leaders must of course fulfill varied responsibilities for engaging all donors, they should be particularly intentional about allocating time, energy and other resources in a disciplined effort focused on that small group of potential philanthropic partners who are in a position to provide transformative gifts. With full appreciation for the need to engage thousands or tens of thousands of constituents in meaningful ways, this book urges that every organization *create a principal gift program focused on 40 potential individual and institutional donors.*

At the core of this book is the assumption that, in organizations small and large in every part of the nonprofit sector, the size of the top 10 gifts—the largest gifts an organization raises—has a tremendous impact. Regular engagement, annual fund and major gift fundraising activity will result in a great number of gifts, and 10 of those will of course be the largest. For those 10 top gifts to be as large as they can possibly be, an organization's efforts with a carefully selected group of potential donors must employ more specialized, customized and resource-intensive approaches.

Many fundraising programs use the term "principal gifts" to denote the largest, most transformative gifts they can elicit. The amount of a principal gift can vary considerably based on an organization's budget—in some organizations a principal gift might total in the range of $10,000, while in another organization "principal" might describe a gift of $10 million or more. Some such gifts will come from individuals and families during their lifetimes. Others will come through estates. Some will come from foundations or corporations. This book focuses on the set of skills, qualities and factors needed for an organization to secure its 10 largest gifts, regardless of source or size.

Some organizations have never pursued a principal gift program, perhaps due to a lack of experience, a lack of time, a lack of confidence or a perceived lack of resources (for example, a feeling that principal gift work can only be done with a dedicated principal gift staff member). While many organizations have employed some elements of the approach to principal gift fundraising offered in this book, few have employed all aspects in a holistic and systematic way. *Raising Your Organization's Largest Gifts: A Principal Gifts Handbook* is designed to help all fundraising leaders design strategies for nurturing the partnerships that will yield their largest philanthropic gifts.

Scale of Success

Board members, presidents, fundraising staff members and fundraising volunteers serve and engage large and diverse constituencies. All members of an organization's community—those who work for the organization and those who are served by the organization—are important to an organization's health and accomplishments. Some contribute time, wisdom, expertise and advocacy. They may have impact through a discovery or an idea, an introduction or endorsement or leadership at a key moment. Others will make essential contributions of financial resources. Annual and multi-year fundraising efforts—whether the goal is measured in thousands of dollars or billions of dollars—depend on many donors giving, each according to capacity. In a healthy fundraising program, some donors will be making first-time gifts, and others will be making their ultimate gifts after years of involvement. Acquisition of new donors and retention of existing donors are essential, not only in increasing fundraising revenue but also in expanding an organization's community of informed, inspired ambassadors and advocates.

At the same time, in most organizations the overall *scale* of success will be determined by a handful of donors making the 10 or so largest gifts. In this book, we'll call these "principal gifts." These very large gifts enable transformational improvements in an organization that can include recruitment of top talent, expansion of facilities, strengthening of programs and even entrance into new and unexplored territory consistent with an organization's mission.

Establishing and sustaining a thriving principal gift program requires attention both to culture and to technique. As the chapters that follow suggest, passion, authenticity and openness to partnership are essential on the part of both donors and fundraisers, but they fall short without specialized attention to donor identification, engagement and relationship building.

Sustained success in securing the largest possible gifts—in and out of campaigns—comes as the result of a sustained and sophisticated principal gift effort, focused on a small number of potential donors. (It is true that not every top 10 gift will come from a person or institutional donor identified and cultivated as a principal gift prospective donor. While surprises in this category of gift are welcome surprises, they are anomalies.) This effort varies from standard major gift fundraising efforts in each stage of the fundraising process:

- shaping of culture,
- identification of potential donors,
- establishment of fundraising objectives,
- allocation of resources including assignment of staff members and other relationship builders, and
- engagement and stewardship.

This book provides detail on these variations.

80-20, 95-5 and the Top 10

I have worked as a professional and volunteer fundraiser with organizations ranging in annual budget from tens of thousands of dollars to several billion dollars. In all these organizations, a large percentage of the money raised has come from a small percentage of donors, and an even smaller number of donors has determined the organization's overall capacity for growth and impact.

When I began my career in fundraising, common wisdom held that 80 percent of dollars came from 20 percent of donors—the so-called "Pareto Principle" or "80-20 rule" applied to fundraising. Over the last three decades, fundraising experts have noted a shift toward a higher percentage of dollars coming from a smaller percentage of donors. In 2015, Bill Levis, project manager of the Fundraising Effectiveness Project that studied thousands of nonprofit organizations, found that 88 percent of gifts came from 12 percent of donors and 76 percent of gifts came from just 3 percent of donors (Levis 2015). In a recent email blast, fundraising expert Jerold Panas noted that his firm Jerold Panas, Linzy & Partners is now finding that 95 to 96 percent of the money comes from 2 to 3 percent of the donors.

For the most part, colleagues tell me they think 80-20 has been replaced by 95-5, and that the new ratio is not likely to change anytime soon. It is important to note, though, that 5 percent of an organization's donors might still include hundreds if not thousands of donors.

In preparing to write this book, I reflected on my own experiences as the architect of several principal gift programs and as a principal gift fundraiser, working with the much smaller number of donors who made the largest gifts in each of the organizations I've served. I reviewed data from the Voluntary Support of Education survey, one of the most comprehensive published surveys that includes data on the impact of top gifts—in this case, the top 12 gifts each year to educational institutions. And I asked fundraising colleagues working across the nonprofit sector to share their own experience.

Data from the 950 educational institutions that responded to the 2016 Voluntary Support of Education survey, conducted by the Council for Aid to Education, revealed these interesting insights:

- On average, the three largest gifts from individuals and families represented 21.4 percent of all giving from individuals and families.
- The three largest bequests represented 59.9 percent of total bequest giving.
- The three largest foundation gifts represented 38.9 percent of total foundation giving.
- The three largest corporate gifts represented 35.1 percent of total corporate giving.
- The 12 largest gifts represented 31.2 percent of total support.
- For both private and public research/doctoral institutions, the 12 largest gifts represented 27.8 percent of total support.
- For private and public master's degree institutions, the 12 largest gifts represented 48.3 percent and 43.3 percent of total support, respectively.
- For private and public baccalaureate institutions, the 12 largest gifts accounted for 46.8 percent and 45 percent of total support, respectively.

In addition, I asked colleagues from across the nonprofit sector—in health care organizations, arts and cultural institutions, and social and community services organizations, as well as in colleges and universities—to provide data, in confidence, on the impact of their top-ten donors. I asked about the impact of these donors on their most recent fiscal year and about the top-ten donors in their most recent campaign. One finding stood out: Although ten donors represented less than 1 percent of the donor base—in some cases .0001 percent of the donor base—*these 10 donors alone contributed between 25 percent and 80 percent of total fundraising revenue.* Even in the largest organizations, with more than 100,000 donors, the decisions of the top 10 were highly consequential. In several cases, they gave 50 percent or more of the total.

Another key finding from my discussions underscores the reality of today's fundraising environment and the importance of a well-designed principal gift approach: *In most organizations, the top three donors accounted for one-third of total dollars raised.* This was true in small arts organizations and in large research universities.

Defining "Principal Gifts"

Prospective principal gift donors are not simply prospective major gift donors with greater wealth. Prospective principal gift donors are those with the capacity and desire—or potential desire—to make an organization one of the primary beneficiaries of their generosity and whose wealth capacity, combined with this inclination toward engaging in philanthropic partnerships, will enable them to make the organization's largest gifts. Most of those who become principal gift donors will give often, over long periods of time. They often will make gifts representing a much larger portion of their wealth than standard major gift modeling would suggest.

An essay by philanthropic expert Robert Sharpe, included in this book as Appendix A, offers further insights. Robert discusses the difference between "regular" gifts, "special" or "campaign" gifts and "ultimate" gifts. He defines "ultimate" gift as "the largest gift a donor is capable of forming the intent to make in support of a particular charitable interest." The focus of Robert's essay is on the *largest gifts donors will make*—during their lifetimes or through their estates—and thus provides essential context to the book's discussion of *an organization's largest gifts.* A donor's ultimate gift may or may not be among an organization's largest gifts. Many of the organization's largest gifts, however, will be ultimate gifts. (Appendix E discusses key differences between major and principal gift fundraising.)

Some of these ultimate gifts are made through estates in the form of bequests. About 15 percent of the largest gifts made in the United States over the past 10 years, for example, came through bequests. In most cases, the decision to include an organization in an estate plan demonstrates a donor's desire to tie an organization to their identity, to their life's work and their greatest values. Principal gift fundraising allows an organization to identify and appropriately cultivate high-capacity donors with the greatest likelihood of linking their legacy with that organization—of making the ultimate expression of their generous commitment to the organization and its future.

Robert's essay also makes the critically important point that most of the largest gifts that come from individuals and families over the coming decades will come from baby boomers. These individuals started turning 70 in 2016, reaching an age at which regular attendance at events and participation in boards and councils begins to diminish even though individuals may have decades of life still ahead. As the population ages, principal gift programs must include robust engagement activity aimed at individuals in their 70s, 80s, 90s, and even early 100s.

About This Book

Raising Your Organization's Largest Gifts: A Principal Gifts Handbook is written for nonprofit board members, current and emerging nonprofit leaders and all staff members and volunteers involved in fundraising. The book provides guidelines that draw on my experience and that of colleagues who have led successful principal gift programs in a variety of organizations. Its lessons apply to organizations large and small, in every part of the nonprofit sector—education, health care, arts and culture, social and community services and beyond. I hope that these guidelines inspire some organizational leaders to introduce a principal gift program. For those who have a program, I hope these guidelines renew, inform, refine and strengthen the results of commitments already made.

My last book, *Belief and Confidence: Donors Talk About Successful Philanthropic Partnership*, described—largely in the words of leading philanthropists— 16 types of belief and confidence that are strong among donors and staff members in the most successful fundraising programs (Schiller 2015). Highly active board members and donors shared with me details of their most satisfying transformational and major gift experiences and highlighted the factors that distinguish these experiences and the motivations behind them.

Building on the lessons recounted in *Belief and Confidence*, this book serves as a strategic guide for those responsible for identifying, engaging and securing philanthropic investments from those donors capable of making an organization's largest gifts, providing practical advice on the special attention and approaches required to ensure that these gifts are as large and consequential as possible.

The book is in seven chapters:

- **Chapter 1** examines organizational culture and the importance of building and sustaining a culture that embraces the concept of philanthropic partnership and is marked by high levels of belief and confidence among donors, organizational leaders, staff members and volunteers. It also discusses the joy that such a culture brings to donors and fundraisers. Appendix B includes reflections from principal gift fundraisers about the impact of such a culture on their own careers.

- **Chapter 2** focuses on identifying prospective principal gift donors. Of all those capable of making what are, for the organization, major gifts, how do we identify those few who have the greatest potential to make the organization's largest gifts—the gifts that in most cases will determine the success or failure of a fundraising campaign? Chapter 2 includes a discussion of the number of prospective principal gift donors that will be required to reach an organization's goals.

- **Chapter 3** discusses the importance of establishing objectives shared between organizations and donors. This chapter draws on the lessons of *Belief and Confidence* and the concept of philanthropic partnership and presents specific ideas from successful principal gift fundraisers and leading philanthropists on how to create shared commitment to outcomes that results in investments representing the largest portions of a principal gift donor's philanthropy.

- **Chapter 4** is about big ideas. Most of an organization's largest gifts are made in response to ambitious, visionary plans. A lack of big ideas is usually the result of lack of sufficient confidence on the part of organizational leaders, not lack of donor capacity to support big ideas.

- **Chapter 5** deals with relationship builders. Relationships between organizations and their top donors typically involve many relationship builders. This chapter discusses the number and responsibilities of these individuals and the support they need to succeed in their roles.

- **Chapter 6** focuses on the special and customized forms of engagement and stewardship required in working with principal gift donors and prospective donors.
- **Chapter 7** focuses on authenticity. In response to both of my previous books, *The Chief Development Officer: Beyond Fundraising* (Schiller 2013) and *Belief and Confidence*, colleagues have observed, and I wholeheartedly agree, that an underlying theme and the single most important quality to success as a chief development officer and as a facilitator of philanthropic partnerships is *authenticity*. Without that quality, sustained success in principal gifts fundraising is simply impossible.
- **Appendix A** is an essay contributed by Robert F. Sharpe Jr., a leading authority on gift planning and a friend and colleague of many years. Underscoring the importance of paying attention to baby boomers in principal gift fundraising, Sharpe's essay complements and provides additional context for this entire book.
- **Appendix B** contains reflections from principal gift fundraisers on "A Joyful Career in Philanthropy."
- **Appendix C** provides a checklist summarizing the key markers of a successful principal gift program.
- **Appendix D** provides components and considerations related to position descriptions for those involved in staffing principal gift efforts.
- **Appendix E** gives a snapshot summary of key differences between major gift fundraising and principal gift fundraising.

Focus and Discipline

In an ideal world, organizational leaders and fundraising staff members would cultivate, solicit and steward every donor in a highly personal, customized way. Whether donors give $1 or $1 million, they deserve recognition and thanks for their generosity. Yet no organization can justify the cost of a development program large enough to solicit and thank every donor in person, let alone allocate the time of the organization's president and board chair to build a one-on-one relationship with every donor. Nor will every one of an organization's donors wish to make that organization one of the top recipients of their giving.

Organizations allocate limited resources across a variety of online, mail, telephone and in-person engagement activities. Some of these tactics are targeted to groups, some to individual donors. Most organizations have major gift programs in which more personalized approaches are deployed, and in which presidents, board members and other top donors are more deeply engaged. Raising an organization's largest gifts—and making sure those gifts are as large as they can and need to be—requires an especially intense focus and discipline that must be understood, embraced and sustained by leadership across the organization.

I have been involved in doubling or tripling fundraising for several organizations, and I have observed the exceptional work of several close colleagues in leading similar efforts for other organizations. In every case, improved retention of donors at all levels was an important factor, as was acquisition of new donors. But the most important factor was the introduction of a principal gift approach and commitment to a culture of philanthropic partnership, shared across leadership, that dramatically increased the size of the ten largest gifts. In addition to producing significantly more fundraising revenue, this transformation raised levels of belief and confidence that in turn drove increased engagement and giving at all levels.

While many organizational leaders believed dramatic increases in fundraising would only come as the result of acquiring new donors at the highest giving levels, the principal factors in transformative growth in giving were changes in approach and culture. For the most part, the donors who went on to make substantially larger gifts to a specific organization were already in that organization's database—some had made top-ten gifts, though at lower levels, and some had not been top donors at all. I won't suggest that any fundraising work is easy, but the changes were relatively simple and straightforward, and the results were profound.

My hope for this book is that it will help readers map their own success in securing gifts that have a transformative effect on their organizations and that allow their most capable donors to give generously and with great satisfaction.

Chapter 1

CULTURE

Sustained success in raising gifts at the highest levels begins with creating and nurturing a culture that encourages and supports *philanthropic partnerships*. Donors make most, if not all, of their largest gifts to organizations that embrace them as partners. Recognizing this, successful fundraisers view their work as *facilitating* the generosity of *partners*, rather than separating donors from their money. This culture of partnership is greatly strengthened when individuals throughout the organization understand and embrace their responsibilities for contributing to high levels of donor *belief and confidence* in the organization.

The Concept of Philanthropic Partnership

For some donors, $1,000 might constitute a large gift. For others, that threshold might be $100 million. When donors decide to make an organization one of the primary beneficiaries of their giving, it is important for the organization to recognize and respond to that expression of philanthropic partnership, regardless of the size of the gift. It is not always possible to know who these donors will be, especially if the largest gift they are capable of making is a relatively small one for the organization. Nor is it an easy matter to focus significant organizational resources on every one of these individuals. Every philanthropic partner is exceptional, however, and organizations must do everything possible to identify these donors and appropriately recognize the importance of their special commitments.

When they are so recognized, these kinds of donors typically talk about the organizations they support in the first person rather than the third person. They derive great pride and satisfaction from their affiliation, and they inspire others as a result. These donors *are* the organization, as much as any president, board member, faculty member, physician or orchestra member. Embracing such donors, not as outsiders but as essential partners in creating the future of the organization, is the starting point for establishing a culture that will yield the largest possible principal gifts.

Two Views of Fundraising

Many people view the job of fundraisers, at its core, as moving money from people who have it and would prefer to keep it to organizations that need it. This view produces denigrating remarks commonly heard by fundraisers such as, "Here comes so-and-so, hold onto your wallet!" It also causes many nonprofit volunteers and non-fundraising staff members to assert, "I'll do anything for the organization as long as I don't have to raise money." This view of fundraising and fundraisers is generally rooted in distaste—no one wants to twist the arm of another, especially a friend. Believing that fundraising involves asking potential donors to do something they don't want to do or, even worse, to do something they will find painful, leads to frustration and burnout among staff members as well as among volunteer fundraisers.

Those who see fundraising as *facilitating philanthropy*, by contrast, sleep much more peacefully and have long and happy careers in fundraising as paid staff or as volunteers. These facilitators assist philanthropists in doing something these donors *want* to do: voluntarily invest some of their time and money back into society through nonprofit organizations. These types of fundraisers see their roles as helping generous donors succeed in being generous—making possible gifts that donors view as successful, meaningful, satisfying and even fun.

Fundraising of any kind—annual gift fundraising, major gift fundraising and principal gift fundraising from individuals, corporations and foundations—is much more successful and enjoyable for everyone concerned when its focus is on facilitating a mutually rewarding experience for donor and organization rather than just about moving money from those who have it to those who need it. The more transactional approach may work in some annual and major gift fundraising, but it simply will not work in principal gift fundraising, especially for sophisticated donors with the greatest giving potential.

Belief and Confidence

Every person engaged with an organization has the capacity both to strengthen and weaken belief and confidence in the organization among its constituents. The higher the levels of belief and confidence among donors, organizational leaders, fundraising staff members and volunteers, the more likely that philanthropic partnerships will thrive and fundraising efforts will reach their full potential.

My last book, *Belief and Confidence: Donors Talk About Successful Philanthropic Partnership*, contains stories from donors that illustrate the importance of 16 types of belief and confidence and offers suggestions about how to strengthen each type. While improving belief and confidence strengthens fundraising at all levels, maximizing principal gift revenue depends upon high levels of belief and confidence across all 16 types.

Existing high levels of belief and confidence in an organization on the part of an individual prospective donor may suggest greater readiness on the part of that donor to be included among those who receive attention from the organization as a potential source of a principal gift. Conversely, low levels of belief and confidence might suggest that a prospective donor warrants different prioritization. In some cases, however, a low level of belief or confidence on the part of a donor or group of donors with great wealth capacity may instead suggest the need to focus greater resources on improvement in belief or confidence rather than removing them from the list of prospective principal gift donors.

The 16 types of belief and confidence listed below are reflected throughout this book:

- *Belief in the importance of giving.* In addition to wealth capacity, top prospective donors have a demonstrated philanthropic spirit.
- *Confidence in personal financial circumstances, present and future.* Prospective donors have confidence in their personal financial circumstances and in their ability to make and fulfill large pledges.

- *Confidence in other personal circumstances.* Prospective donors have confidence in personal circumstances such as health, family stability and time to focus on philanthropy.
- *Belief in mission.* Top prospective donors are strongly aligned with the organization's mission.
- *Confidence in leaders.* Prospective donors know and have great confidence in multiple organizational leaders—administrative and board.
- *Belief in vision and confidence in strategy.* Prospective donors understand and are excited by the vision of organizational leaders, and they have confidence in strategic plans. Many will have played a role in shaping the vision and especially in shaping strategies to implement the vision.
- *Confidence in organizational financial planning and stability, present and future.* Prospective donors have confidence in the organization's financial leaders, financial plans and financial future. This does not mean they believe the organization does not need fundraising revenue; rather, they have confidence that financial resources are managed well and used wisely.
- *Confidence in the capacity to raise additional funds.* Donors know that others will join them in supporting the organization.
- *Widespread belief that the organization is worthy of philanthropic investment.* The CEO, executive team members, board members and other organizational leaders believe that the organization is prepared to use a large gift wisely.
- *Confidence among the organization's leaders.* The CEO, executive team members, board members and other organizational leaders believe in each other and have confidence in each other's leadership, vision, strategy and planning.
- *Confidence in the fundraising staff.* Organizational leaders also have confidence in the chief development officer and in the fundraising staff and program.
- *Confidence in setting and meeting ambitious goals.* Leaders have ambitious strategic objectives and confidence in the organization's capacity to meet fundraising goals associated with those objectives.
- *Belief in philanthropic partnerships.* The CEO, executive team members, board members, and other organizational leaders embrace their roles in philanthropic partnerships. They believe that donors are essential partners in creating the future of the organization.

- *Staff belief in the organization's work.* Staff members throughout the organization believe in the mission, and donors see that staff members share their belief.
- *Staff confidence in the organization's leadership.* Staff members throughout the organization have confidence in leaders, plans and goals, and potential donors see and are encouraged by that confidence.
- *Fundraising staff believe in the value of their work.* Staff members believe that their individual contributions make a difference.

Self-Solicitation

Philanthropic partners with high levels of belief and confidence will often talk about their largest gifts as "self-solicited." They come to feel a degree of ownership of the organization, responsibility for its future and a depth of understanding about the organization and its priorities that give them the confidence to make transformational investments, in many cases without needing to be asked. As I wrote in the introduction to *Belief and Confidence*:

> The most striking finding in my discussions with leading philanthropists, and notable in its prevalence, is that almost every major and transformational gift described as highly satisfying and/or most successful was also described by the donors as *self-solicited.* Exploring this donor perspective further, with both donors and with organizational leaders most deeply involved in work with top donors, it became clear that environments marked by high levels of belief and confidence produce philanthropic partnerships: a culture in which both organizational leaders and donors talk about each other as partners. There is no "us and them." And philanthropic partnership *blurs the line between solicitation and self-solicitation.* There is rarely a moment of asking because the depth of partnership often makes the "ask" irrelevant.
>
> "Most of our gifts have been self-investigated and self-initiated," says philanthropist Dennis Keller, speaking of his family's giving, that has included nearly a dozen eight-figure gifts. "The best way, that has the happiest reverberations for philanthropists and organizations, is to encourage deep engagement through which philanthropists figure out what they want to do based on their core beliefs and informed desires to help."
>
> Jason Franklin, philanthropist and Executive Director of Bolder Giving, agrees. "Gifts can be both solicited and self-solicited at the same time.

Engaged donors develop an intention to give before an "ask" is even articulated. In many cases they will express this intention before anyone makes an "ask." And even when the subject is raised by a solicitor, in the donor's mind the gift has already been made."

A Joyful Experience

Beyond producing the best fundraising results, a culture of philanthropic partnership also produces what Dennis Keller calls "the happiest reverberations for philanthropists and organizations." Donors make gifts that satisfy their personal objectives and that have the impact they desire. The gifts are both meaningful and successful. Organizations excel in fulfilling their missions and expanding their impact. Professional fundraisers, too, feel these reverberations, and they experience much greater job satisfaction as a result. (I asked some of the principal gift fundraisers I admire the most for their thoughts on this subject; their reflections can be found in Appendix B.)

Summary

Dennis Keller's quote underscores the importance of a culture that embraces the concept of philanthropic partnership and is marked by the highest levels of belief and confidence. His and his family's giving—along with the giving of hundreds of engaged and generous philanthropists—makes clear that the central question in working with philanthropic people is not "will they give?" but "how much and to whom?"

Donors make their largest gifts to organizations in which they feel ownership. They embrace the organization and are embraced as partners. They and the organizations they support accomplish things together that neither could accomplish separately. Staff members work with them as facilitators, assisting them in making gifts that work—gifts that make sense for the organization and for the donor and that bring great satisfaction to both. Donor belief and confidence grow deeper, leading to larger investments and inspiring large investments by other donors. A mature culture of philanthropy emerges, capable of supporting the largest gifts the organization needs and can use wisely, and capable of securing the largest gifts its top prospective donors can make.

Chapter 2

IDENTIFICATION

Whether operating in a mature culture of philanthropic partnership or in an organization that is in the process of establishing or transforming its culture, the first step in the fundraising process is to identify the prospective donors on whom to focus principal gift attention. Considerations include the number of potential donors appropriate for this focus, criteria for selection and roles and responsibilities of those charged with making the selection and regularly updating the list.

Number of Prospective Principal Gift Donors

As we have discussed, an organization's top handful of gifts account for a significant percentage of total fundraising revenue. This book uses "top 10" instead of "handful," but in actuality there is no magic number—an organization might raise 50 percent of one year's total from one donor, or 80 percent from the top three donors or 60 percent from the top 10.

Based on my experience and that of my colleagues, I would suggest identifying approximately 40 prospective donors for the type of principal gifts attention outlined in this book. Focusing on 40 should mean that most of the top 10 gifts made each year come from donors who have been engaged in the ways outlined in this book—as prospective principal gift donors.

One reason for choosing 40 as a target number is that it is standard practice in development to create gift tables that assume a yield of one gift per three to five prospective donors.

Another reason is that in my experience working with several presidents, board chairs and development committee and principal gift committee chairs, I have found that 40 is the number of potential principal gift donors—individuals, families, foundations and corporations—that someone in a leadership role can keep top of mind. A higher number means that the list probably won't get the regular attention it deserves. Having a lower number means that less money will be raised than might otherwise be possible.

Does this mean that an organization cannot or should not have a principal gift program that identifies 100 or 200 prospective donors at that organization's upper tier of giving? Not necessarily. A program with that many prospective donors, however, must function like a "large major gift" program. There won't be sufficient time for the CEO, board chair and other senior leaders to focus on all prospective donors of principal gifts and to engage them as deeply as necessary. Spreading attention evenly across so many potential donors will dilute the quality of engagement for all. A large principal gifts program is not bad in and of itself. But every organization should still identify and have a different stance and approach toward those forty or so potential donors who are the most likely to make the organization's largest gifts. In the case of a large, existing principal gifts program, this might mean creating a small group of prospective donors within the larger group. This discipline will ensure that those largest gifts are as big as possible. It is worth noting that when this happens, all gifts, including other major gifts, often also increase in size, as overall levels of confidence grow and as organizational leaders and donors see the organization as worthy and capable of handling larger gifts.

This is not to suggest that organizations without this type of focus won't receive large gifts. Rather, by focusing on approximately 40 donors as potential sources of principal gifts, the organization can make the 10 largest gifts even larger and, in doing so, increase its overall success in fundraising. Without such a focus, resources will either be spread too thin—resulting in nothing more than a "large major gift" program—or leaders will not be pushed to devote sufficient time to the largest gifts. The result might be the nurturing of only a handful of principal gift philanthropic partnerships where dozens might have been possible.

Three Criteria for Selection

Most fundraising programs rate prospective donors by wealth capacity and by inclination. Principal gift fundraising also requires attention to philanthropic priority.

Wealth capacity. A great deal of information about a prospective donor's wealth capacity can be found online and through research and wealth screening services that access publicly-available information, such as real estate holdings and business ownership. Still more information is available through giving histories, including donor lists of other organizations, and by asking donors directly about their past and current giving and their future philanthropic plans. The more donors are treated like partners, the more likely they are to reveal their capacity to support an organization's strategic plans—especially when they have participated in the planning and are excited to implement the plans.

Common practice in assigning wealth capacity ratings is to use or at least begin with 5 percent of visible wealth. For example, someone with known wealth of $100 million might be rated $5 million, with an assumption that they have the capacity to give $1 million per year for five years. While this information is useful and usually accompanies wealth screening data, it is generic and formulaic—it represents an average behavior rather than the behavior of someone who is among an organization's principal philanthropic partners. The level of philanthropic priority a donor assigns to an organization can greatly increase or decrease the percentage of wealth a donor is willing to focus on that organization.

A common mistake is to give too much weight to wealth capacity. Nearly every organization I've served had Bill Gates and Oprah Winfrey on their top prospective donor list. Yet, in most cases, these high-profile philanthropists had neither existing relationships nor any indication of interest in the organization. When I did have occasion to dig into the history of how they were placed on the list of prospective donors, I inevitably found that they were mentioned in some brainstorming session focused on identifying potential donors. I even heard one well-meaning volunteer suggest that the door might be opened through a relative of the chef of one of these potential donors!

Wealth does not predict belief in the importance of giving or propensity to give. Bill Gates and Oprah Winfrey are philanthropic, even if they do not belong on the principal gift prospective donor lists for most organizations. Some wealthy people, however, are not philanthropic at all, and never will be. Others are still building wealth and are reinvesting in their own companies and will contemplate serious philanthropy only later in their lives. Still others are busy raising children, or working every hour of the day and night, or both, leaving little time for the type of engagement that leads to the largest gifts. The most philanthropically minded of these will start giving—often through buying tables at events of organizations where family members or friends are more involved—but they are unlikely to make their largest gifts until they are ready to be involved.

The "wealth capacity" rating for an institutional donor is typically more straightforward. Foundations and corporations will usually publish or, through giving behavior, show the scale of giving they are willing to consider. Even so, foundations and corporations have been known to jump to significantly higher levels of giving when engaged in a major project or initiative aligned with their interests, often in partnership with other donors.

In short, when it comes to identifying those with the greatest overall capacity for principal gifts, wealth capacity is important but it's only a beginning.

Inclination. Potential donors must have high inclination toward giving to an organization in order to warrant consideration as a potential principal gift donor.

Giving-inclination ratings are based on a gift officer's assessment of the current level of willingness and readiness of donors to make a gift. Board members, donors with a long history of giving and donors who have told an organization that they are planning to make a gift will have a high rating. Donors who have expressed dissatisfaction with an organization's plans or leadership or have asked to be removed from an organization's mailing list usually will have a low rating.

Inclination ratings are less widely used and more subjective, unless the indication of inclination comes directly from the prospective donor. Even then, the information may lead to inaccurate projections. For example, donors may have high inclination for a specific objective that is not currently a priority of the organization, or high inclination to make a gift in the future, but low inclination toward a large gift in the near-term for a current strategic objective. The larger the gift, in terms of a percentage of the donor's wealth, the more likely that the timing of the gift will depend on personal circumstances of the donor rather than organizational timelines such as fiscal years or campaign deadlines. Again, inclination to support the organization may be high, but inclination to make a large gift in the near term may simultaneously be medium to low.

Philanthropic priority. Most significantly, inclination usually fails to take *philanthropic priority* into account. A donor with $100 million in net worth and high inclination will likely be "rated" $5 million during the planning for a major campaign. When the donor makes a gift of $50,000, the organization might assume that the donor was not inspired by the campaign objectives, didn't relate to leadership or wasn't properly cultivated or solicited. In many cases, however, the explanation is simpler: the organization is not a high priority in the gift planning of the donor and the donor's family. They may, in fact, be highly impressed by the organization's leaders and vision but have several other organizations they consider to be more important in their philanthropy.

Philanthropic priority can be changed through information, education and engagement. It will also change as the priorities of individual and institutional donors evolve. When identifying potential principal gift donors for today, organizations need to know where they rank among the current priorities of potential donors. They must also understand the factors and likely timing involved in improving their position of priority.

Wealth and inclination do not necessarily translate into priority. Wealthy people, especially those known to be philanthropic, are routinely presented—some would say bombarded—with giving opportunities. They may have high ability and inclination to support dozens of institutions, but rarely will they give more than a few organizations gifts that represent a substantial percentage of their assets.

In addition to prioritizing their giving, donors *scale* their giving. A donor with $100 million, high inclination and a $5 million capacity rating may consider the local animal shelter to be their highest philanthropic priority. In a $5 million campaign for the shelter, however, they are unlikely to make a gift of the full amount of the campaign—even with evidence of capacity, inclination and high priority. Donors are likely to study the prospective donor list for the campaign, expect that others will do their share and then assess what is needed from them to make the campaign successful. They might well determine that $1 million would be the right scale of gift for them and for the shelter.

Organizations also inadvertently lower sights of donors by lowering their own expectations: If the largest giving opportunity listed in the animal shelter's campaign brochure is $500,000, the same donor might give $500,000 instead of $1 million. In short, organizational leaders should not assume that someone with high wealth capacity, inclination and philanthropic priority for their organization will make a gift larger than the donor believes is needed and will be used wisely by the organization.

I recently discussed principal gift prospective donor identification with a leading philanthropist and good friend. In that discussion, he offered a succinct phrase that captures this idea beautifully: "Organizations need to know the difference between people who want to hug them and people who simply want to shake their hand." He spoke about several organizations he supports, explaining that some are in the "hug" category—they are among his philanthropic priorities for very specific reasons. Others are in the "handshake" category, meaning he admires their work, loves supporting them and will continue doing so, but he will never "hug" them.

Gathering Information on Inclination and Priority

Gathering sufficient information to make wise decisions about the prospective principal gift donor list may seem daunting, but one of the best sources of information on inclination and priority is too often overlooked. Donors and potential donors are generally reluctant to share information about their personal wealth. Questions about inclination and especially about philanthropic priority, however, are likely to produce informative and even enthusiastic responses. Fundraisers who ask donors to talk about their priorities for giving and gift planning, and what they most want to accomplish with their philanthropy, accomplish several things:

- They let donors know that they think of them as giving and generous people.
- They show interest in the donors' philanthropic objectives and respect for their philanthropic choices.
- They gain information on how donors make giving decisions.
- They learn about other institutions that rank high in donors' philanthropic planning and why.
- They learn where their organizations stand in the overall philanthropic thinking of donors.

Furthermore, information received directly from donors is almost always more accurate and more persuasive to colleagues when planning cultivation and solicitation activities.

I have attended hundreds of prospective donor strategy meetings involving development staff members and sometimes organizational leaders and board members. Donor objectives are sometimes known and addressed but, for the most part, an unspoken assumption guides the process: namely, that organizational representatives need to determine (and usually argue about) what the donor should support and then present "giving opportunities" to the donor. The corollary assumption is that donors don't know what they want to support—they need organizations to figure it out for them, or at least start the conversation.

If fundraisers are to be facilitators first and foremost, as they should be, then donor objectives must be known and factored into prospective donor strategy discussions from the beginning. This is especially true with prospective donors of principal gifts with whom an organization aims to develop a long-term philanthropic partnership. The assumptions outlined in the previous paragraph are completely wrong: Donors *do* have objectives and have thought about what they want to accomplish with their philanthropy.

Learning that an organization is not a philanthropic priority for a donor and understanding why helps an organization determine who belongs on the current top 40 list. Having that critical knowledge enables an organization to develop a better list of donors who in fact are prospective principal gift donors. It also leads to better strategies for engaging with those who might later be added to the list. Further, asking donors additional questions about the most enjoyable gift experiences they've ever had, and how and why their priorities for giving have changed over time, enhances an organization's knowledge about how to make itself a higher priority for those donors.

Philanthropic people will rarely dodge such questions, particularly if they believe an organizational representative is interested in helping them achieve their philanthropic objectives and not just in eliciting the largest gift possible. Beyond asking about their objectives and listening carefully to their answers, successful principal gift fundraisers demonstrate genuine interest through proper stewardship, reporting on the impact of the donor's past gifts, and being honest when the organization they represent is not the right partner for accomplishing a specific objective. A prominent principal gift fundraiser I know recently sent a donor to another organization much better equipped to be a partner for the donor's highly specific philanthropic purpose. In this case, the fundraiser prioritized honesty and trust ahead of short-term financial gain. In doing so, he strengthened his organization's long-term relationship with the donor.

Broadening the Pool

Belief and Confidence includes quotes from leading philanthropists that clearly demonstrated that mission alignment and impact are more important than prior affiliation when it comes to the largest gifts donors make. Philanthropic partners are much less interested in the dollar goal of a campaign than in the impact the campaign will have on the organization and society and how closely that impact aligns with the donor's own values and objectives.

That is good news for those charged with broadening the pool of prospective principal gift donors. When an organization has a clear and compelling plan for impact and a track record that gives confidence to a potential donor, anyone or any institutional donor with common interests becomes a potential philanthropic partner. Prior affiliation, such as having graduated from the organization or having been a patient, may make opening the door a bit easier. But it is far less important than alignment of purpose and likelihood of success.

Broadening the pool of prospective principal gift donors also can happen within the group of donors who have prior affiliation. A former colleague is doing groundbreaking work in cause-related fundraising within a major university. After years of meeting with an individual who had given generously to the annual fund, he asked about the donor's broader philanthropic objectives. The donor indicated that in addition to the university's undergraduate program from which he had graduated, one of his top philanthropic priorities was Alzheimer's research. The donor was not aware that the university was doing important work in this area. By connecting the donor to that work, my friend greatly expanded the donor's philanthropic partnership with the university.

Three Criteria in Combination

Giving-capacity ratings are essential. They help development programs prioritize the deployment of resources, especially human resources, in the cultivation and solicitation of all prospective donors. They provide a starting point for evaluating candidates for the prospective principal gift donor list.

At the same time, programs that give wealth capacity too much weight waste considerable resources chasing the wrong people. On the flip side, gift-capacity ratings may cause an organization to underestimate the giving potential of a donor for whom the organization is or can become the highest priority.

Giving-capacity ratings are based on averages and formulas, nothing more. There are many cases of extremely wealthy people deciding to give far more than the typical predictive models suggest. Those participating in The Giving Pledge (https://givingpledge.org) are examples. The only way to determine someone's true giving capacity is to develop the kinds of relationships discussed in this book.

Inclination ratings are also important but are rarely useful without additional detail and context—inclination to give what type of gift, what size of gift, in what time frame and in what relation to other giving by the donor?

Priority is easier to measure than inclination and, combined with giving capacity, likely to produce more accurate annual giving and campaign planning projections. Donors who have given an organization high priority should themselves receive high priority attention, and they are among the most important sources of information about how to raise an organization's priority level among other donors. The more donors are treated as partners, the more likely they are to reveal their thinking about an organization's priority in their philanthropic planning.

While giving capacity by itself can sometimes lead organizations to waste time on wealthy people who do not show the inclination and potential to make an organization a philanthropic priority, long shots do occasionally pay off. A prospective donor with significant capacity—especially someone with a proven track record of making very large gifts—might be worth a closer look simply because of the scale of their demonstrated philanthropy.

That said, organizational leaders are too often tempted to believe that the largest potential donors are unknown to the organization—that they must be discovered through better research, better development leadership, better information. My experience proves something different: almost every donor who will make a top 10 gift in the next five to 10 years is already known to the organization. Whether they had some affiliation with the organization before giving or began their relationship through shared philanthropic objectives, most have been regular donors or volunteers or both by the time they make a top 10 gift. The principal contributing factors to growth in the size of the top 10 gifts will be culture and stance toward these donors as philanthropic partners, focus on prospective donors with the best combinations of the criteria above and types and depth of engagement.

Older Donors

According to the *Chronicle of Philanthropy*, 55 percent of the 50 largest gifts made in the United States in 2016 came from people 70 and older. Six of the top 50 gifts came from people 90 and older. Baby boomers began turning 70 in 2016 (Di Mento and Singh 2018). The number of individuals reaching the age when donors typically make decisions about their largest gifts is growing. The age distribution of potential individual donors will vary by type of organization, but most organizations will be dealing with a more elderly population of prospective principal gift donors than in the past.

As philanthropic people get older, they gain a better understanding of how much they will need and how much they can give away, potentially increasing the amount they will allocate to charitable gifts. As they age further, or when a spouse dies, they may also shift giving plans from revocable (such as a bequest intention) to irrevocable (cash, appreciated assets, trusts and so on). Robert Sharpe, an expert in gift planning, elaborates on these points in the essay in Appendix A of this book.

Few organizations do a good job of sustaining their engagement with older donors who are no longer interested in serving on a board or able to attend gatherings and events. Older donors may drop out of top annual-giving societies due to changes in income streams. Organizations must guard against overlooking these "off the radar" older donors.

Roles and Responsibilities

The chief development officer has the primary responsibility for driving the identification process. A variety of perspectives will assist the chief development officer in making the best possible choices for the top 40 list, and in keeping that list accurate and up to date.

Researchers and analysts, front-line gift officers involved in individual giving (including planned giving) and corporate and foundation giving, the CEO, board leaders and other principal gift donors should all be involved in selecting potential principal gift donors. The chief development officer—or, where possible, someone assigned by the chief development officer to focus on the maintenance of this list and tracking of activity with these 40 potential donors—should regularly consult with all the individuals who are in the best position to identify potential donors. These key contributors and fundraising professionals should meet as a group at least once a year to review and refresh the list.

One objective of regular review, which will be reinforced by engagement strategies discussed later in this book, is to keep these 40 donors "top of mind" for all key leaders. The CEO, board chair, development chair and chief development officer, at a minimum, should know who is on this list and be thinking about the list *on a weekly basis.*

Summary

The chief development officer should begin by identifying 40 prospective individual, corporate and foundation donors, engaging key principal gifts program stakeholders in the process of nominating candidates for the list, reviewing candidates against criteria for inclusion and refreshing the list on a regular basis.

Criteria for inclusion should begin with wealth capacity but should not stop there. They must also include inclination to support the organization *and* to make the organization a philanthropic priority. Successful programs pay careful attention to donors already in their database.

Through regular review and updating of the list, these 40 remain top of mind for key fundraising leaders, especially the CEO, board chair, development chair and chief development officer. This top-of-mind status leads to and is reinforced by the engagement strategies outlined in the following chapters.

Chapter 3

SHARED OBJECTIVES

Many nonprofit organizations were launched by a single philanthropist or a small group of philanthropists. These generous people had or were inspired by an idea and combined their resources with the assets of others—various types of expertise, perhaps some land set aside by community leaders and so on—to get the organization off the ground.

Leaders of organizations with successful principal gift programs recognize that donors are, always have been and will continue to be essential partners in creating a nonprofit organization's future. These leaders cannot possibly involve every donor in planning at every level, but they seek wisdom, expertise, and ideas from individuals beyond those currently on the payroll, and even beyond those on the board.

The Donor Life Cycle and Shared Objectives

One of the earliest illustrations of the life cycle of the donor relationship that I learned was "the five I's"—identification, information, interest, involvement and investment. That life–cycle model is usually drawn as a circle. Donors typically enter at "identification," although they may also enter because of a shared interest, or through a gift, even before they are identified by the development program. Information leads to greater interest, interest to greater involvement, involvement to greater investment of gifts and giving—especially if properly stewarded—to deepened interest, involvement and yet more giving.

In annual and major gift fundraising, an organization establishes strategic objectives, establishes fundraising objectives in support of those strategic objectives (not all strategic objectives require fundraising revenue) and then aims to inform potential donors and build their interest. Where possible, organizations gather information on the philanthropic interests and objectives of potential donors and target information and interest-building activity to create matches between donor and organizational objectives. The more a potential donor identifies with and shares the objectives discussed in an appeal, the more likely they are to give.

For donors designated as "prospective major gift donors" and assigned to frontline fundraising staff members, information on donor objectives can be gathered in face-to-face visits. Such visits can also be used to inform donors about plans that might spark interest in expanding their philanthropic objectives. Equipped with this information, development officers can tailor gift proposals. In some cases, an objective expressed by a donor with high capacity and readiness to give may encourage a slight shift or reprioritization in an organization's strategic objectives. Alternatively, it may suggest further engagement and information aimed at bringing the donor's objectives into closer alignment with organizational objectives that have a greater chance of making the donor's gift as successful as possible.

For a smaller number of potential major gift donors, involvement at some point in the planning process—through surveys, participation in focus groups, service on advisory councils or even a seat at the strategic planning table—introduces an opportunity to deepen donor excitement and buy-in and thus increases the likelihood and scale of philanthropic investment in the plan.

For prospective principal gift donors, *a seat at the table is essential.* Information must flow in both directions and to a much greater degree. Through relationships built with multiple organizational leaders, and through engagement that gives these potential donors a deeper understanding of the challenges and opportunities facing the organization, prospective principal gift donors develop personal ownership of strategic objectives while they are being formed. These donors often play a role in shaping those objectives, adding their unique perspectives and expertise that may result in more informed and compelling plans.

Involvement in Planning

In my research for *Belief and Confidence,* I found, as Jerry Panas did when writing *Mega Gifts,* that most of an organization's largest gifts come from board members, former board members and families of board members, or from corporations and foundations with an employee or trustee on the board of the organization (Panas 2005). It is no surprise that this is true, given board members' involvement in the planning process.

Prospective principal gift donors may or may not want to serve on a board, and some may not be appropriate for board membership. The potential to establish shared objectives is much higher for board members, however, and principal gift program leaders must think carefully about how to replicate that level of engagement in planning and plan implementation for non-board prospective donors. This is not just a question of access to planning—they must also be sufficiently educated to ensure that their objectives can be brought into alignment with the organization's mission and values and the current vision of administrative and board leaders. One such engagement that can be effective is to add a prospective principal gift donor to a board's investment committee or a long-range planning committee without requiring full board membership.

Timelines Are Not Always Relevant

Organizational timelines and donor timelines are not the same. As one moves from annual giving strategy to campaign and major gift strategy to principal gift strategy, organizational timelines become less relevant while donor timelines become more important.

In annual giving, the fiscal year is extremely important. While a donor may or may not pay attention, the organization creates strategies designed to hit a goal within a specific time frame. The timeline typically does matter when it comes to impact (not just dollar goals), because the organization's ability to perform its core work with a balanced budget depends on reaching targets set for the annual fund.

In campaign and major gift fundraising, timelines are also important. Campaign timelines create deadlines—some real and some artificial—that drive donor decision making. An example of a "real" deadline is a capital project, such as when an organization decides it will not break ground on a new building project until a specified amount is raised. An example of an "artificial" deadline is a comprehensive campaign target with a campaign end date. In this case, the organization prefers to raise a certain amount of money in a certain amount of time, but the reality is that a specific project under discussion with a donor would not fail if the donor's gift was made the day after the official campaign ended.

In building both a culture of philanthropic partnership and specific philanthropic partnerships, it is critical that organizational representatives never prioritize artificial timelines above shared objectives. If the shared goal is to establish a carefully designed challenge gift to support recruitment and retention of top physicians and inspire nine other donors to respond to the challenge, for example, the fiscal year or the campaign end date may be entirely irrelevant in the mind of the donor. Fundraisers are always under fiscal-year and campaign-timeline pressures, but allowing these timelines to shortcut the full flowering of a shared objective can lead to a reduced gift or a damaged long-term partnership. This is true in major gift fundraising and is especially true in principal gift fundraising. Before talking about a timeline, principal gift fundraisers would be wise to ask themselves, "Is this timeline truly relevant, or am I losing sight of potential long-term gain by responding to my own short-term pressures?"

In addition to timelines that threaten full development of a shared objective, organizational timelines can also simply be out of sync with donor timelines. When a donor making a large gift needs to time the gift to the sale of a business, or needs to delay a decision until an annual family foundation meeting, for example, an organizational timeline is just not as important. Pressuring a donor to give a gift before they are ready demonstrates lack of commitment to true partnership.

Dollar Targets Are Not Shared Objectives

Organizational leaders who think that hitting a fiscal-year fundraising goal or a campaign goal is as exciting to a principal gift donor as it is to them need to think again.

This does not mean that senior administrative leaders allow top donors to dictate strategy—a fear commonly expressed by organizational leaders who lack experience in building effective philanthropic partnerships. It does mean that leaders must take sufficient time to build trust and to educate potential philanthropic partners about the variety of factors that have brought leaders to their current conclusions. They need to listen and be open to ideas they may not have considered that could strengthen planning and outcomes.

Giving donors this seat at the table, a voice in the planning process, creates shared ownership of goals. This level of engagement often leads donors to begin to talk about plans in the first person—"our" strategic plans rather than "your" strategic plans. As illustrated through many of the stories shared in *Belief and Confidence,* donors with this level of involvement often don't even need to be asked for a gift. In that book, I included a relevant quote in that regard from philanthropist Dennis Keller:

> "Most of our gifts have been self-investigated and self-initiated…The best way…is to encourage deep engagement through which philanthropists figure out what they want to do based on their core beliefs and informed desires to help."

When donors are fully invested in the plan intellectually and emotionally, their financial support follows naturally and even joyfully.

Shared BIG Objectives

Those with the capacity to make an organization's largest gifts, if engaged properly, inspire leaders to greater levels of ambition, even as leaders inspire those donors to greater levels of philanthropic partnership. Top donors give leaders confidence to develop big ideas and to engage their colleagues in contributing to those ideas. In many cases, prospective principal gift donors will make contributions beyond inspiring confidence and making large investments, including offering professional expertise and valuable perspectives as business, community and philanthropic leaders. The next chapter focuses on what is possible when a shared-objective approach is taken to the highest levels of ambition and achievement.

Chapter 4

BIG IDEAS

Raising large gifts requires big ideas. Sometimes donors will initiate big ideas. In other cases, they will wait for organizational leaders to articulate bold vision, shape ambitious plans and demonstrate confidence in achieving those plans. Regardless of the source of the vision, large gifts follow big ideas, not the other way around.

Shaping Big Ideas

Big ideas may emerge from annual planning, but more likely they will grow out of organization-wide discussions, such as those that take place in long-range planning, and out of discussions with leading donors and potential donors. Some of these ideas will be transformational—they will substantially increase or improve an organization's capacity to serve its constituents. Others will strengthen infrastructure—creating new facilities or building endowment, for example. Ideas that inspire the largest gifts are framed as outward-facing rather than inward-facing—they focus on donors and organizations coming together in ways that substantially strengthen an organization's impact on its constituents and on society, rather than more narrowly on how a donor can meet an organization's needs.

Laura Simic, vice president for university advancement at Boise State University, offered this excellent advice. She digs for the biggest idea associated with every giving opportunity by asking, "So what?" A colleague says he needs money to buy a new piece of equipment. "So what?" The colleague explains that the equipment will support faculty members and students and allow them to advance their research. "So what?" The colleague explains that the research will contribute to a drug discovery process aimed at treating a currently untreatable disease. "Aha—there's the big idea."

This approach is important in major gift fundraising, but it is critical in principal gift fundraising. Big ideas begin with creative, confident and ambitious thinking about an organization's potential for significant impact. In shaping big ideas, the "why" precedes and is more important than the "what."

"Why?" Before "What?"

A theater company leading with "What?" determines, through strategic planning, that it needs a new building. The building will cost $40 million. A quarter of that amount is available through a combination of cash reserves and loans, but $30 million must be raised. The organization creates a list of giving opportunities that includes naming the building with a gift of $15 million. The staff designs a beautiful brochure and fundraisers start meeting with donors who have capacity and potential interest in such a naming opportunity. The theater's two largest gifts in the past 10 years were $5 million and $4 million, respectively.

While such an approach might result in a $15 million gift, it is different than a partnership approach that is much more likely to yield a gift that, for this organization, would be transformational.

In shaping the big idea—in leading with "Why?"—the chief development officer and other leaders first ask themselves, "So what?" The theater company has been operating out of rented space for years. The organization is no longer able to accommodate a growing and highly engaged audience. Existing audience members want a nicer lobby and a place to enjoy food and drinks at intermission. Organizational leaders want to be able to provide proper backstage accommodations to a higher caliber of visiting artists. A large rehearsal room is needed.

Aware of two board members and five other audience members with principal gift capacity and a real passion for the theater, the chief development officer and CEO inform them of the theater's aspirations and ask if they are willing to participate in the planning process. Several agree, and one of them suggests expanding the rehearsal room to accommodate after-school instruction for local children with an interest in theater, an idea that is enthusiastically embraced by the artistic director. Senior leaders determine that the benefits far outweigh the incremental costs. The chief development officer and CEO understand that in suggesting the expansion, the planning committee member has increased her ownership of the project. Perhaps she will even agree to name the rehearsal room or the after-school program.

As the plans take shape, that committee member becomes so excited about the project that she asks for a meeting with the CEO and declares that she would like to make the naming gift for the building. Her motivation is not only the impact that the new building will have on the community, but also the impact that her gift will have on the giving of others.

I had the great privilege of taking part in the development and funding of a big idea at the University of Chicago. The university sought to remove the crippling burden of loan debt from low-income students—debt that was preventing many highly qualified students from considering a University of Chicago education, even with a scholarship grant that covered tuition. Other expenses—such as room, board and travel—required these students to accept a daunting level of loan debt that was impossible for them and their families to justify. In part, the "So what?" or "Why?" in this case was making high-quality education available to more low-income students. But the bigger "Why?" was predicated on the university's desire to assemble the best, brightest and most diverse student body to create the strongest possible educational environment and to change lives. Rather than raise one endowed loan-relief fund at a time, the university partnered with a generous anonymous donor to design a $100 million gift that replaced student loans for every low-income student for a period of decades. The university promised to raise, during that period, the money required to endow the loan-relief program in perpetuity. Thousands of donors have been inspired to support the permanent endowment. Every university would be happy to add $100 million to its scholarship endowment, but the lead objective should not be "$100 million" or "more endowment." Those are answers to the question, "What?" The answers to the question, "Why?" are the ones that truly inspire large gifts.

Relative Terms

"Large" and "big" are relative terms. For one organization, a big idea will require a large gift of $5,000, and for another $5 million. For a few organizations, "big" ideas will require gifts in the tens or hundreds of millions.

David Dunlop was a pioneer in the field of principal gift fundraising and established the principal gifts program at Cornell University. When I first met him, Dave served as the manager for Cornell's relationships with 22 families—a radical idea at the time, when major gift fundraisers were typically assigned 100 to 200 families. As one of my principal mentors, Dave taught me that multi-year campaign pledges were typically 10 times the size of annual gifts, but that a donor's largest gifts—sometimes made in response to a transformational idea, and sometimes as an ultimate gift at the end of life—could easily be a thousand times the size of an annual gift. Those 22 families would eventually give billions—not just millions—to Cornell.

My experience has been the same. I have routinely seen donors give $10,000 to an annual fund and then give $100,000 or more to a campaign. I've also seen these donors give millions or tens of millions to a shared objective developed by the donor in concert with the organization in a culture of philanthropic partnership. Without big, shared objectives, the same donors might continue giving at the $10,000 level for years or decades without any indication that they might be prepared to do more.

Donors scale their giving. In a campaign to raise $2 million for new and exciting upgrades in medical technology, a donor capable of making a $10 million gift would not likely give $2 million. The donor might give $1 million, or even less, challenging others to give the rest.

Collaborations Between Organizations

One way for organizations with relatively small budgets to shape a larger vision is to collaborate with other organizations. For example, several arts organizations could propose the transformation of an entire downtown cultural district. One of my favorite examples of philanthropic partnership, involving collaboration among multiple organizations and a donor, is Joan Kroc's transformational giving to public media.

In the early 1980s, American philanthropist Joan Kroc began giving to her local public media station, KPBS. In 1996, she gave the station $3 million toward construction of new studios. Stephanie Bergsma, a development professional at KPBS, eventually suggested that Kevin Klose, president of National Public Radio, meet the McDonald's heiress, knowing that NPR and KPBS together could present a vision for public media much larger than KPBS could do on its own. Klose and Bergsma recounted to me that, shortly before Kroc died, she told the NPR president, "We're really going to do something great together." They did not know how successful they had been in presenting a transformational idea until Kroc died. Upon her death, she left $5 million to KPBS—its largest gift ever—and $200 million to NPR. The gift would not have happened without these two, separately incorporated nonprofits reaching across organizational boundaries to shape an idea that inspired a completely different scale of philanthropic investment.

Obstacles

The principal obstacles to big-idea fundraising include these:

- Lack of confidence on the part of organizational leaders in the capacity of donors, causing leaders to doubt that funds would ever be available to support big ideas;
- Lack of a process for generating, vetting, and approving big ideas;
- Lack of confidence on the part of organizational leaders or donors in the capacity of an organization to implement a big idea;
- Lack of willingness to partner with donors and, in some cases, with other nonprofit organizations; and
- Lack of truly big ideas—specifically, lack of ideas that are viewed both by organizational leaders and by donors as significant and transformative.

These obstacles reinforce each other. Lack of confidence in donor capacity, for example, leads to lack of willingness to invest time and energy in creating big ideas. Lack of big ideas diminishes donor confidence in an organization's capacity to use a large gift wisely.

Start With Organizational Leaders

Even with a level of engagement in planning sufficient to inspire self-initiated gifts and the confidence to make large gifts, donors will not typically make gifts larger than those required to meet defined objectives. In other words, donors are unlikely to push organizational leaders to levels of ambition beyond where the donors perceive that leaders are willing and able to go.

"Donors are usually the easiest when it comes to sight-raising," says Curt Simic, president emeritus of the Indiana University Foundation. "Getting an organization's leadership to raise their sights must be accomplished first.

Otherwise, donors will sit on the sidelines or gravitate to other organizations with bold vision and leadership."

In every organization I've served, and in every organization my friends have served, lack of capacity in the existing donor base was not the issue. I have yet to find an exception. Regardless, board leaders, administrative leaders and development officers are too quick to conclude that insufficient donor giving capacity is the problem. Much more often, driven by that conscious or subconscious lack of confidence in donor capacity, leaders refuse or neglect to take the first step of articulating or soliciting ideas that would drive the largest gifts. The lack of large gifts becomes a self-fulfilling prophecy.

Organizational leaders also need confidence in the power of those ideas to inspire large gifts. A friend and truly ambitious fundraising leader shared the following recent experience: "I met with a generous couple to talk about a new gift. They had been engaged with the organization and were genuinely excited about our plans and the level of our ambition. I asked them to consider a gift 20 times the size of their largest gift to date. When they called to respond, they thanked me for my visit, told me how happy they were to participate, but told me I had asked for the wrong amount. My heart sank. Then they told me they planned to give double what I had requested. Their gift made them one of the five largest donors to our campaign—I had completely underestimated the role they wanted to play in bringing our big ideas to fruition."

Overcoming Lack of Confidence

In one small music organization I know, the largest gifts each year were in the $1,000 range. For some donors, this was a large gift, but many consistent donors had significantly greater giving capacity. Organizational leaders felt that a $1,000 gift in the context of an annual $150,000 budget was "large." Revenue, however, was falling short and the organization was headed toward closure. A few donors, understanding that gifts at the $2,000 level would allow the organization to continue attracting world-class artists and that gifts at the $5,000 level would allow the organization to commission new musical works on a regular basis, started talking about these bigger ideas. Many donors responded at these higher levels. Nearly all of these donors had already been contributing and likely could have given $2,000 or more in earlier years, but the organization had not articulated the impact that gifts at higher levels would have. For this organization, attracting world-class artists and making important contributions to the greater chamber music repertoire were big ideas, even though the gifts required were measured in the thousands rather than millions of dollars.

In another organization, leaders initially wanted to leave an eight-figure gift out of the totals of a campaign's nucleus fund, "since the gift is an anomaly, and in counting it, we might set too high a goal for the public phase." That big gift had been inspired by a big idea—transformation of an entire program that had involved months of dreaming and planning on the part of one department. But the organization's top leaders still saw the size of the gift as something that could not again be achieved. After a second eight-figure gift was received—largely in response to another big idea—the same leaders not only counted the gift in the campaign, but they began focusing more on shaping and soliciting ideas that would drive a third gift, and more after that. The philanthropic capacity of the organization's donors and potential donors had not been the challenge—it was a lack of confidence in raising larger gifts, combined with a lack of big ideas driven by such confidence. Once confidence was gained, big ideas flowed and large gifts followed.

In one institution, when I asked leaders for ideas for gifts an order of magnitude larger than previously raised gifts, many told me I was wasting their time, that such gifts would never happen and we were simply spinning wheels. One even threw in a few expletives for good measure! Nonetheless, we went on to shape ideas that drove individual gifts as large as the entire fundraising totals of earlier years.

When the University of Chicago began articulating $100 million ideas, a donor stepped forward. Another donor followed with a $300 million gift. The university has gone on to raise several additional nine-figure gifts, and many more eight-figure gifts, all driven by big ideas and confidence on the part of organizational leaders and donors.

More Than Multiplication

Multiplying one number by another to create a bigger number does not create *an idea* that inspires a larger gift. Four endowed chairs in an orchestra, each $1,000,000, do not constitute a $4 million giving opportunity. A donor may respond positively to a request to fund four endowed chairs, but they are responding four times to the same idea. If, on the other hand, organizational leaders want to increase the orchestra's ability to attract and retain the best musicians, and they have determined that 10 endowed chairs plus an international touring fund would enhance the orchestra's standing as a world-class ensemble and contribute to the city's global reputation, then the organization has defined a $15 million idea.

My colleagues and I once worked with a donor who quickly accumulated an enormous amount of money through a highly successful business. He was asked, for several years in a row, to consider giving a $2 million gift—40 times the size of his largest gift to date. Although he was philanthropically minded and easily capable of making such as gift, he wasn't inspired by the idea. Our new president met with the donor, and they got into a deep discussion about philanthropy and its role in strategic decision-making. The donor asked for an example, and the president shared one that was on his mind because he was preparing for a board discussion on the topic: The organization needed to make a strategic decision between two options related to a new facility— one that would cost $25 million more than the other. The president and other senior leaders believed that the more expensive option was by far the better choice in terms of impact on those served by the organization. In the context of other expenses facing the organization at the time, however, and because the project had to proceed without delay, he expected the board and administration would choose the less expensive option. Although this was one of the first meetings between the president and this donor, and even though no solicitation had been planned, the donor's immediate response was, "I can do that!" He was inspired by a big idea, one that he knew only he and few others could support. This donor and his family could have made a dozen $2 million gifts, but that was not at all the same to him as partnering, with a $25 million gift, to make a big idea come to life.

Endowment

When the concept of "big idea" comes up, related to fundraising, leaders often jump immediately to endowment. If an organization's annual budget is $10 million, and if its largest gifts are typically $100,000, it's easy just to do the math and say that a $20 million endowment gift would provide the organization with a dependable income stream of approximately $1 million per year. Voila—a $20 million idea!

Gifts to endowment are important, but appeals for large endowment gifts must involve big ideas that go well beyond simply having more money in the bank. Donors are rarely inspired by a request that is mostly about making the organization wealthier.

This does not mean endowment opportunities need to support *new* expenses. A gift that endows a new expense is appealing, of course, because the donor sees change and growth and knows that they have allowed for that enhancement to continue in perpetuity. But endowing current positions and current scholarships often works just as well because donors feel their impact on people's lives even while they are improving the long-term financial position of the organization.

Sophisticated donors often develop strong feelings about endowment. I've worked with donors who will give only to endowment, and others who are passionately opposed to gifts of endowment. Reasons are widely varied— some who favor endowment feel that organizations become too dependent on annual operating revenue by adding facilities without long-term assets to support maintenance, for example. Others oppose endowment because they feel they can build wealth much more quickly—and have more to give in the long run—by reinvesting in their own companies rather than placing funds into the typically conservative investment portfolios of nonprofits. Knowing a donor's feelings can help a fundraiser avoid having a discussion derailed before it even gets going.

As Robert Sharpe points out in his essay in Appendix A, donors who make large gifts during their lifetimes rarely give to unrestricted endowment. Most of the largest endowments have been built in large measure with unrestricted endowment gifts made through bequests.

Donors Who Lead by Example

When it comes to an organization's largest gifts, some donor must be the first one to establish a new level of giving. This is often someone very close to the organization—someone who is already one of the largest donors, someone who is on the board or a foundation with a deep interest in funding a major initiative to inspire others to join in support. Those who have been lead donors before are likely to be among those who do it again at yet higher levels.

Those who have served as lead donors in the past are also excellent candidates for membership on the principal gift steering committee, or at least for an advisory role in the principal gift process. They have done something that the organization wants to replicate and can provide valuable information about what inspired them to do so.

In establishing a new level, donors raise the sights of colleagues and friends who see themselves in the same category of capacity and affinity. They influence these peers to think about the organization in a different way—on a different scale.

Board members are among the best candidates to take the lead in raising the philanthropic bar. It is important that at least some of them do so, because potential donors outside the board pay attention to the giving of board members. They know that board members have more knowledge than they do about quality of leadership, vision, planning, financial management and the readiness of an organization to implement ambitious ideas. When board members with known capacity for high-level gifts do not make philanthropic investments consistent with their capacity, the confidence of others in doing so is greatly diminished.

One organization launched a campaign seven times the size of its previous campaign. The plans were clear and compelling, and the board was 100 percent supportive. But the scale of ambition was daunting until a board member, who was already the organization's largest donor, stepped forward with a gift almost seven times the size of his family's largest previous gifts. This set the tone. Several other board members did the same, followed by donors not on the board.

The lead donor is a rare and precious donor; those who take this step should be celebrated! When one institution or individual is not prepared to step up to a new level alone, an alternative strategy to consider is asking several donors to create the new level together—"If we can get two others to make a commitment of X, will you also make a commitment at that level, helping the organization raise the sights of all prospective donors?"

The first gift at a new level is always the hardest; the second can be equally difficult. But the third is much easier, and gifts beyond the third are significantly easier to secure. This is because donors have shown that they—not just the organization's leaders—believe the organization to be worthy of such gifts. They have enough confidence in leaders, vision and strategic and financial planning to justify a gift at the new level.

Donors Rarely Go It Alone

Donors who do take the lead still prefer to have other donors accompany them. Even if they make the naming gift for a project, they like the idea of other donors joining them and want to play a role in inspiring greater participation. A philanthropic partner I know well recently self-solicited in a campaign, making a lead gift in support of an organizational priority that she knew would be the hardest sell to other donors—maintenance of a facility. She asked what would be required, gave half, and worked with the organization to raise the other half. The other half came from more than 200 donors. This was exceptionally meaningful to the lead donor—not only because her gift inspired a total amount that was double her gift, but because it inspired many others to give, including some who may become future lead and principal gift donors.

Another donor, in response to an exceptionally ambitious but very carefully developed plan, made a gift 1,100 times the size of his previous gift. But that amount was half of the total cost of the vision. In making the gift, he made clear his intention to work with organizational leaders to engage thousands of other donors in giving the rest. He did so, and he went on to give much, much more to a project that has become a major part of his life's work.

Summary

Large gifts rarely precede the ambition, careful planning and confidence associated with big ideas. Big ideas come first. Big ideas inspire large gifts, and large gifts inspire big ideas that in turn inspire more and larger gifts. Donors, given an opportunity, will often initiate or contribute to big ideas. In other cases, they will respond to the big ideas of other donors or of organizational leaders. They will look for organizational leaders who are confident and ready to follow through on big ideas. Confidence among leaders inspires confidence among donors and vice versa. When donors choose to partner at a new giving level, they inspire confidence in other donors, and this inspires greater confidence in leaders to develop more big ideas.

I have never encountered an organization that was not capable, with proper leadership and guidance, of developing ideas that would drive gifts at least twice as large as any the organization had ever received. Usually, the organization and its donors have the capacity to shape reasonable giving opportunities 10 or even 100 times the size of its largest past gifts.

My favorite quote related to big ideas is that of the great architect and visionary designer of the World's Columbian Exhibition of 1893, Daniel Burnham, who said: "Make no little plans; they have no magic to stir men's blood and probably themselves will not be realized. Make big plans; aim high in hope and work." With that in mind, I urge all fundraisers to make big plans and aim high in the vital work of nurturing partnerships that can lead to principal gifts and all the good that such gifts do for organizations and society.

Chapter 5

RELATIONSHIP BUILDERS

Principal gift fundraising is substantially different from major gift fundraising in the number and variety of relationship builders required, the degree of involvement of senior leaders and roles and responsibilities of those involved.

Number of Relationship Builders

In annual gift fundraising, the number of organizational representatives required to support an effective donor-organization relationship might be one, two or three at most. These might include an annual giving staff member, a peer donor and perhaps a representative of the part of the organization for which the donor has greatest affinity.

In major gift fundraising, the number of organizational representatives required is between two and four. It should not be one, because the relationship between donor and organization can be lost altogether, or at least lost temporarily, with the departure of a major gift officer or president or the death of a board member or peer donor. When the engagement of a group of major gift donors depends on just one person, that person's departure can set back fundraising activity for months or years.

In principal gift fundraising, the approach to relationship building is entirely different. The number of organizational representatives involved must be significantly larger—at least three, and often seven or more. The variety of individuals involved is more pronounced, and the support and coordination of relationships is more complex and more important.

Annual fund donors might be engaged a few times each year, and usually in groups rather than one-on-one. Major gift donors might be engaged monthly. Principal gift donors, however, should be engaged several times per month, on average. This engagement will involve multiple people. It will be coordinated and consistent, with all members of the *relationship building team* complementing and building upon each other's work in strengthening the relationship (see below for detail on the critical importance of coordination and the crucial difference between control and coordination). An engagement might be as simple as calling the donor for advice or to share some news, or it could be as extensive as having the donor participate in a multi-day retreat.

Assuming three interactions per month with each principal gift donor and 40 prospective donors, 120 meaningful engagement steps a month need to be planned, coordinated, tracked, and shared with those involved in the relationship. That is six per workday. Given all the responsibilities shouldered by today's chief development officer, I strongly advise having someone assigned to assist with this effort. This could be a frontline principal gift officer or a high-level administrative assistant. Alternatively, the chief development officer could distribute responsibilities among several staff members and then coordinate their work. Even with the best of intentions, careful principal gift planning and coordination are likely to get pushed to the back burner by the burning issue of the day—such as a human resources problem, an upset board member or a call from the president's office with an urgent request for information.

Relationship Building Personnel

In major gift fundraising, the buy-in of senior leaders across the organization is important. Senior administrators and board leaders will often need to play an important role in the cultivation and solicitation processes. They must be available, have high levels of belief and confidence in the organization and be able to inspire belief and confidence in donors.

To maximize the size and impact of the ten largest gifts, buy-in of senior leaders and their active participation in relationship building are both *essential*. That is especially true for the CEO, board chair, campaign/development chair, chief program officer (provost/dean, artistic director, chief of surgery, etc.) and chief development officer. Even the most inspirational CEO or the most dynamic chief development officer cannot do this alone.

In relationship building, senior leaders will rely on the support of staff members, some of whom will have their own relationships with principal gift donors. Their work will also benefit inestimably from the involvement and example of peer donors.

CEO

The chief executive officer will be involved, to at least some degree, in every prospective principal gift donor relationship. For some donors, this relationship will be the primary relationship. But all principal gift donors will want some relationship with the CEO and will need confidence that the CEO is committed to the success of the program or person being supported by their large gift.

In large organizations, the CEO may have little day-to-day involvement with the project or area being supported by a principal gift donor, but the donor knows that few major initiatives succeed without the support of the CEO. Initiatives almost always require resources beyond those covered by a gift, and donors know the CEO has authority over decisions related to those resources.

In organizations of all sizes, CEOs have many demands on their time, and attention to principal gift relationships—as important as it is—is only one. Furthermore, many demands on the CEO require immediate attention. While an impending gift decision may be considered "pressing," most relationship-building work falls into the category of "sustained and steady attention required."

CEOs are also in demand by every constituency of an organization, internal and external. This includes many donors beyond those identified as prospective principal gift donors. Given these other responsibilities, CEOs with whom I have worked and spoken agree that 40 is a large but reasonable number of top potential donors to keep "top of mind."

Board Chair

The board typically has ultimate responsibility for governance and financial planning and management. The board typically hires and fires the CEO. Given that the board chair is the leader of the board, top donors often want a relationship with the person in that role, usually regarded as the highest role in the organization. They may want to know that the board fully supports the current CEO's vision and strategies, or they may want assurances about the overall financial direction of the organization, including the board's plans with respect to cash reserves and endowment. Sometimes they simply admire the person in this role and want, through their major philanthropic investment in the organization, to have a closer relationship with that person and possibly with the whole board.

Other Senior Administrative Leaders

Given the impact of principal gifts on fundraising totals and the fundraising program overall, the chief development officer must be involved in all principal gift relationships, even if playing a largely supporting role to the CEO or another senior leader. In addition to direct involvement in relationship building where appropriate, the chief development officer is instrumental in implementing and guiding the principal gift fundraising program. More on the chief development officer's role follows later in this chapter.

Chief financial officers are often important contributors, sometimes as regular members of the relationship team, and sometimes as contributors only at specific moments, such as giving a donor or a donor's adviser a detailed picture of an organization's financial health or plans. Some donors want a great deal of detail, especially when making large and complex gifts. Chief financial officers can provide not only detail but also organizational context, historical context and a perspective different than that of the CEO or chief development officer.

Depending on the focus of the gift under discussion, donors may value the perspectives of the leaders who will be most directly involved in utilizing or implementing the gift—for example, the head of oncology, the curator of contemporary art, the head of the rare books collection, a distinguished faculty member, the administrator of the scholarship program or the person in charge of hiring and training the front-line service providers.

A significant part of my work as chief development officer was at universities, and faculty members were invaluable partners in building strong relationships with prospective principal gift donors. Faculty members were often hesitant to get involved in fundraising at first, often saying, "I don't feel comfortable asking for money." I would explain that fundraising was much more about building confidence, and that they didn't need to play any role in an actual solicitation. I would ask them, "Do you have confidence in your

Academic

department and your colleagues, and do you think the donor will be proud of a gift in this area?" The answer, of course, was always "yes." With that context, we identified the basis for the faculty member's role as a relationship builder. I can't begin to count the number of faculty members who became enthusiastic "fundraisers" by doing something they enjoyed and did exceptionally well: sharing their passion for their research, their teaching and their students.

Other Board Leaders

The development committee chair, the campaign chair, a development committee member, a board member with shared philanthropic interests or a board member with a personal or business relationship with a donor may make an excellent addition to the relationship building team.

Other Principal Gift Donors

In all types of fundraising, peers provide invaluable support to fundraising efforts. They lead by example, they instill confidence, and they open doors. This is especially true in principal gift fundraising. If they believe in their role as facilitators rather than arm-twisters, then they want to share the success and joy they have experienced in giving with other philanthropically minded individuals.

As mentioned above, when an organization is raising the level of top gifts, the hardest gift to secure at the new level is the first one. That wonderful person or institution who provides that first gift goes out on a limb, believing that the organization is truly ready to partner at that higher level. The second gift at the new level is also a challenge, because many people will consider the first an anomaly. Once the second is secured, momentum builds. The third is much easier to raise, and then a new level is established. In such circumstances, donors who have already given a principal gift can play an effective, perhaps even essential, role in persuading others to give at that level. Someone who has already donated at the principal gift level can reassure a prospective principal gift donor that a requested principal gift is not out of scale. Further, when this reassurance comes from a known and respected friend or colleague, the confidence of the prospective donor is substantially higher than if the other donor is unknown to the prospective donor.

Other Staff Members and Volunteers

The relationship building team may benefit from the perspective of other staff members and volunteers who:

- have an existing relationship with the donor;
- have special expertise in an area of great interest to the donor;
- bring expertise in deferred–giving instruments;
- bring perspective or expertise that enhances stewardship of earlier gifts and of the relationship; or
- will be a key beneficiary of the gift under discussion.

One common mistake is to make stewardship an afterthought. Stewardship experts—those charged with ensuring gifts are used properly, assisting in tracking and reporting on the impact of gifts and recognizing gifts appropriately, for example—need to be included from the beginning, and stewardship planning should be a part of the discussion long before any large gift is broached.

Coordination Is Critical

Principal gift relationship-building involves many people. Philanthropic partnerships that have been in place for many years often involve dozens of relationships—including relationships that may never be known to the chief development officer and other organizational leaders.

Trying to control all these relationships is folly. Chief development officers or CEOs who insist on reviewing and approving every interaction with a principal gift donor create unnecessary and counterproductive bottlenecks. Furthermore, such an approach is disrespectful to donors and antithetical to partnership.

Coordination of relationships, however, is critically important. While generous donors appreciate access to various constituents—senior leaders, those most involved in using their gifts and those who benefit from their gifts, for example—they do not want to be assaulted by multiple people from the organization making uncoordinated and inappropriate requests for support. As partnerships deepen, they often expand. For example, at the University of Chicago we found that 71 percent of our top donors had supported multiple parts of the university. These multi-faceted relationships strengthen partnerships and donors' understanding of what is most needed and when, but they also increase the number of people who will hope to leverage a personal relationship into a gift for their individual project or program.

Senior leaders may be tempted to restrict or even quash such relationships. That only limits a donor's sense of being intimately involved. Most organizational representatives will respect a thoughtful institution-wide strategy when they understand their role and the long-term benefit of the coordinated strategy to the donor and the organization, even when this means that a request in support of their department or favored project is deemphasized. At the same time, donors are grown-ups—they will know how to handle the occasional rogue solicitor, especially when they've come to trust that organizational leaders are doing their best to facilitate smooth and productive relationships across sometimes highly complex or large organizations.

The Principal Gift Steering Committee

Though many individuals are typically involved in building the partnerships that lead to principal gifts—the more the better, in my view—every principal gift program needs a steering committee that includes top leaders and has staff support.

The CEO, chief development officer and at least one senior board leader— board chair, vice chair who focuses on development, development chair, campaign chair, principal gift chair or nominating committee chair—form the *principal gift steering committee*. These three or more senior leaders know the name of each family, foundation and corporation on the top 40 list. They know key information about these prospective principal gift donors and are aware of the status of the organization's relationship with each.

Steering committee members must keep these prospective donors top of mind. They have their phone numbers and email addresses at hand. When there is good news to share, they think about who on the list would welcome receiving that news from a senior leader, prior to a public announcement. When there is bad news, they talk about how sensitively and appropriately to inform top 40 donors to provide context and diminish negative repercussions. They regularly review and update engagement strategies including the membership of relationship-building teams. They also regularly review and revise the top 40 list.

In short, they accept responsibility for driving strategies aimed at creating the strongest possible philanthropic partnerships that lead to the largest possible gifts from prospective principal gift donors.

Roles and Responsibilities of the Chief Development Officer

Steering committee members, including the chief development officer, have many demands on their time. They will see the value of their principal gift steering work, but other professional and personal responsibilities—including daily crises—will distract them from regular, careful, thoughtful attention to principal gifts. Members of the steering committee therefore need to be able to rely on someone to keep them on task. That role is largely the responsibility of the chief development officer. Chief development officers have many other responsibilities (see *The Chief Development Officer: Beyond Fundraising* for detail drawn from more than 60 interviews with leading CDOs), but this may be the single most important. The size of an organization's top 10 gifts will determine the overall success or failure of fundraising efforts and, in turn, determine the overall success or failure of strategic plans. CEOs and board members share in responsibility for the success of fundraising efforts, but chief development officers are likely to be held most accountable.

Another important role of the chief development officer is to monitor and adjust, as needed, the makeup of the team of relationship builders working with each prospective principal gift donor. Teams need to include the right mix and number of senior leaders, staff members and volunteers. They also need to include individuals who will be a good match for the prospective donor, taking into account perspectives and personalities.

Chief development officers need to establish a plan for regular communication with the steering committee. This will vary by institution and will involve a mix of face-to-face meetings, telephone conferences, regular written reports and email updates that is most appropriate for the organization and the committee. I would suggest at least a quarterly face-to-face meeting for the full group, and more frequent face-to-face interactions between chief development officer and CEO, and between chief development officer and involved board members. The chief development officer must own the responsibility for keeping the steering committee active and on task, and for meeting the deadlines established by the committee.

It is also important for the chief development officer to work with the CEO and board chair to keep other relevant board leaders engaged and informed if they are not members of the steering committee. This is especially true for the chair of the nominating committee, given the role that board recruitment and membership play in the deep engagement of principal gift donors and prospective donors.

Chief development officers also need to own responsibility for the day-to-day management associated with the principal gift program, even if they delegate to trusted members of their staff. Principal gift work requires excellent research, writing, scheduling, coaching, stewardship and many other tasks and associated skills. The chief development officer must ensure that all such support is available and properly resourced.

Roles and Responsibilities of Staff Relationship Managers

Given the many responsibilities of today's chief development officers, the support of staff relationship managers is invaluable. Chief development officers who insist on shouldering full responsibility for coordinating strategies and managing relationship-building teams for all top prospective donors create bottlenecks, delay progress on strategy development and implementation and often fail to keep relationship builders adequately engaged and informed.

CEOs and board leaders will expect chief development officers to be well informed about prospective principal gift donors. Not all the standard duties of a staff relationship manager (sometimes called prospect manager) can be assigned to another person. Chief development officers should participate in strategy conversations and meet regularly with the person or people serving as staff relationship managers for all prospective principal gift donors. That said, chief development officers should delegate significant responsibility for developing draft strategies, shaping and updating relationship-building teams, creating briefings and proposals, following up on requests from relationship builders or promises made to the donor by those relationship builders, stewardship activity and so on. The chief development officers may elect to take on these responsibilities for a small number of prospective principal gift donors—serving as staff relationship manager for the board chair and campaign chair, for example—but doing so for 40 prospective donors will almost certainly be a mistake.

Another aspect of individual giving that cannot be overlooked is that the larger a gift, the more likely it is that it will involve assets and structures other than cash, such as trusts. Related to this, donors are often capable of making gifts larger than they think they can make, unaware, for example, of instruments that allow them to defer or reduce taxes on assets ultimately designated for charitable purposes (such as charitable remainder trusts). Chief development officers and relationship managers either need knowledge of how to listen for and act upon information that suggests a donor's willingness to give surpasses the level of their perceived capability, or they need team members, such as planned giving experts, involved in the relationship or involved in strategy who can add that knowledge into the equation.

Creating the Right Infrastructure for Raising Principal Gifts

In terms of building the right internal structures to ensure success in securing principal gifts, two additional considerations are paramount.

First, the best structure eschews silos in favor of an organization-wide approach. Principal gift fundraising is not one person's job, nor one department's job. In an organization of a certain size, a principal gift approach might warrant the creation of a principal gift officer position or department whose charge will be to support an organization-wide principal gift approach. In many organizations, however, it does not require a dedicated position at all. It is first and foremost a mindset—an organizational approach or stance that must be embraced and promoted by all senior leaders—especially the CEO, board chair, development/campaign chair and chief development officer—with widespread understanding across the organization, including among principal gift prospective donors themselves.

Second, a word of caution. The cost to secure a large gift from an existing donor will be much, much smaller than the cost to acquire a brand-new donor making a relatively small first gift. This may tempt some organizational leaders to focus all fundraising efforts on the largest gifts. Sustained success in raising large gifts, however, requires attention to fundraising and a robust pipeline of donors at all levels. Large gifts may produce a stronger return on investment, but organizations failing to invest in donor acquisition and gifts at the base of the giving pyramid—the smallest gifts an organization receives—do so at their own peril. Tomorrow's largest gifts, in many cases, will come from donors whose giving relationship begins at a modest level and is nurtured over decades.

There are some troubling signs when it comes to the future of principal gift fundraising. Gifts from the wealthiest donors are increasing, while gifts from lower-income donors have declined significantly in recent years. According to a report from the Institute for Policy Studies (Collins, Flannery and Hoxie 2016), itemized charitable contributions from the top 1 percent of income earners in the United States increased 57 percent between 2003 and 2013. During the same period, itemized charitable deductions from donors making less than $100,000 declined by 34 percent. While total giving by Americans has reached record levels in recent years, fewer Americans are giving to charity, according to an analysis conducted by the *Chronicle of Philanthropy* (2017). "In 2015," according to that analysis, "only 24 percent of taxpayers reported a charitable gift…That's down from 2000 to 2006, years when that figure routinely reached 30 or 31 percent." The report states that "Donations from households earning $200,000 or more now total 52 percent of all itemized contributions. In the early 2000s, that number was consistently in the 30s."

The report also gives some specific examples of organizations that are moving away from costly, lower return-on-investment donor acquisition while investing more in fundraising efforts aimed at larger gifts. This is consistent with observations colleagues and I have made. One colleague, Don Hasseltine, former vice president for development at Brown University, is quoted in the report pointing out that leaders often "can't resist the more immediate payoff of adding principal-gift officers…not thinking about 25 years down the line." In some cases, organizations making the shift were paying too little attention to major gift fundraising, and some degree of shift was appropriate. Each organization must find its appropriate balance. For the purposes of this book, however, I simply observe two things:

- Most of the principal gift donors with whom I've worked talk about the first gift they made, and that first gift rarely has been anything close to a gift the organization would have considered "major."
- Most sophisticated philanthropic partners will not just be pleased that an organization has many supporters at a wide variety of levels, they will *expect* it—and they may even frame gifts as challenge gifts to promote it.

Summary

Relationships with prospective principal gift donors deepen donor engagement and ownership of the organization and its strategic objectives. The more relationships they have, the more donors will feel that they are partners in creating the future of the organization, rather than outsiders.

As philanthropic partnerships develop, relationships will blossom naturally. Attempting to control every dimension of these relationships is a waste of time and energy and shows lack of respect for donors and for colleagues. Communication with those involved, and coordination and support of their involvement, allows partnerships to flourish.

Chief development officers cannot succeed in principal gifts on their own. CEOs and board leaders need to accept their critically important roles and responsibilities related to this work. Chief development officers are, however, accountable for organizational progress and outcomes in principal gifts. They need to position themselves for success by creating and supporting a process for principal gifts that engages all key stakeholders and a structure within the development department that supports their efforts.

Internal partnership leads to stronger philanthropic partnerships. Silos and internal competition weaken principal gift efforts.

Many of tomorrow's largest gifts will come from today's first-time donors, and these donors will more likely start with a gift of $10 or $100 than with $1 million or $10 million. Positive early giving experiences can pave the way for a healthy philanthropic partnership many years in the future. Conversely, negative early giving experiences can lead to lasting bad feeling. Shifting resources away from pipeline-building is a short-term strategy with potentially serious and negative long-term repercussions.

Chapter 6

ENGAGEMENT

The leading philanthropists I interviewed for my previous book, *Belief and Confidence,* told me that more than 75 percent of their largest gifts went to organizations where they or close family members were serving or had served on the board. For some of those philanthropists, 100 percent of top gifts went to organizations connected to their board service. My friend and colleague Kevin Heaney, vice president for advancement at Princeton University, told me that in Princeton's last campaign the top 20 donors, who collectively gave one third of the total raised, had served on an average of eight boards or organized committees at the university. This is consistent with my professional and consulting experience in dozens of organizations, large and small. Deep engagement—the kind offered by board service—matters.

Giving 40 board seats to individuals on the prospective principal gift donor list, however, is not likely practical nor desirable. Giving capacity and philanthropic priority are not the only criteria most organizations use in the board nomination process. It is also true that some of those on the top 40 list will not be interested in board membership. A board must include people whose collective contributions of time, expertise, advocacy and financial resources provide leadership required to help an organization reach its overall aspirations, not just its fundraising goals.

While membership on a board—particularly in an organization with a healthy culture of philanthropic partnership—affords excellent opportunities for deep engagement, there are other options. It is the quality of engagement, more than the seat on the board, that matters for success in principal gifts.

Qualities of Board Engagement

With so much giving tied to board membership, it is worth examining the qualities of engagement offered by board membership. Such qualities can be replicated in circumstances other than board membership for those who are not appropriate for or interested in board service. This examination will also help leaders working in organizations with politically appointed boards, where the lack of opportunity to appoint significant numbers of top prospective donors to the board makes other types of engagement that replicate the experience of board membership all the more important.

One important quality is *access*. Board members have significant access to the CEO and other administrative and programmatic leaders. They also have access to the organization's financial history and financial planning. In developing engagement strategies for prospective principal gift donors, relationship builders should be aware of the benefits of such access and think about how to create similar opportunities.

Another important quality is *involvement in strategic and financial planning and decision-making*. Prospective donors see the finalized public versions of plans, and they may even have an opportunity to see more detailed plans. But board members know much more about strategic and financial planning—they know the reasoning behind decisions to proceed with certain objectives and not with others. Participation in the planning process instills deeper confidence in the outcomes of planning that is hard to gain without that participation. Planning need not be limited in all aspects to board members, however, and principal gift strategists do well to find appropriate ways to engage non-board members in discussions about plans before they are finalized.

Board members develop *ownership* of strategic objectives, and in doing so they develop ownership of associated fundraising goals. Many of them will be involved in setting those goals. In *Belief and Confidence*, donors described most of their largest gifts as "self-initiated" or "self-solicited," and in large measure the self-initiation grew out of this sense of ownership of the plans. Non-board prospective principal gift donors will also respond more generously when they feel some sense of ownership in the plans and objectives of an organization.

With access and engagement in planning comes *regularity of interaction*. Most board members engage with administrative and programmatic leadership, as well as with other major donors, at least quarterly. If they are involved in committees, they probably engage monthly. If they are responsible for strategic planning, or if they serve on an executive committee, they are likely engaged weekly during certain times of the year or periods of intense activity. Keeping all board members engaged is not easy and requires thought, but a certain degree of engagement comes, automatically, with board service. Principal gift strategists need to think about how to create similarly meaningful and regular engagement for non-board members.

Committees and Councils

Committees and councils can be an excellent tool for creating meaningful engagement. They are especially successful when they tap the expertise, intellect, and energy of members. They need not be permanent—sometimes the most effective are ad hoc task forces that are given a clear task, a defined timeline and a required period of intense engagement. No matter how they are structured, committees must have a clear purpose with measurable impact, so that participants feel their volunteer time was well spent.

A word of caution: When faced with the need to engage large numbers of potential donors in ways other than board service, organizational leaders are sometimes too quick to create advisory groups, campaign councils and other committees. Committees are not bad in and of themselves, but they are frustrating to staff as well as prospective donors when they become make-work or when they result in "show-and-tell" meetings in which staff members talk at volunteers. Time is valuable for high-net-worth donors; traveling and then sitting through a presentation that could have been delivered in writing, listening to others talk rather than being engaged in a conversation and participating in discussions in which only a small part of the content is relevant to their individual interests can create more resentment than productive engagement.

Furthermore, membership on a committee or council need not involve group meetings at all. If a member has an important contribution to make, and if that contribution can be made by phone, by completion of an individually assigned task or through interaction with a staff member or committee chair, such participation can be recognized by inclusion on a list of members of a committee or advisory group without requiring any group meetings at all.

In summary, fundraisers should leverage committees and councils, but they must make sure that such bodies have a purpose, measurable goals and requirements for contribution of time that are appropriate to the member and the tasks at hand. They should also ensure clarity of purpose—pretending that support of fundraising efforts is not a primary purpose of a council when it is the central purpose, for example, is dishonest and will backfire. Members of committees and councils should be able to look back on their involvement with pride, satisfaction and a clear sense of accomplishment. This is important for donors at all levels, but it is critically important for prospective principal gift donors.

Customized Engagement

Donors will remember and be proud of one high-impact contribution of time much longer than they will remember one year of service on a board or committee that did not engage them deeply. Deep engagement comes through tapping the full passion, intellect and expertise of a donor. While we can't afford to design and support customized engagement strategies for each and every prospective donor, we can and must create such strategies for prospective principal gift donors.

Customization begins with listening to the donor's desire for engagement. Does the donor have a lot of time available, or just a little? Do they have time every month, or only at certain times of year? Are they willing to travel to meetings? Do they want their spouse or children involved? What do they most want to learn? How do they want to structure their input? What expertise do they have? What are their principal philanthropic interests—in general, and within the organization? Ask them how to inform them. Ask them how to involve them. Ask them how to ask them. Ask them how to thank them. And ask them how to recognize them. Knowing the answers to these questions and more allows organizational leaders to match donor qualifications and interests with an organization's needs for volunteer time and expertise. It also enables donors and organizational leaders to develop authentic and lasting philanthropic partnerships.

Listening once is not enough. Those who are meeting with prospective principal gift donors need to stay close enough to them to know when personal circumstances and interests change. Prospective donors may have a significant change in net worth due to a divorce, the sale of a business, or an inheritance. They may have substantially more time available due to retirement or completing service on another board. They may develop a new interest through a child's hobby, a personal tragedy or a major world event. Regular, active listening and noting information for the principal gift steering committee is tremendously important.

I once had a board member and principal gift donor who felt guilty about his inability to attend board meetings. He served on multiple corporate boards, and these meetings regularly conflicted with our organization's board meetings. He felt he had a lot to contribute, but the timing of board meetings kept him from making those contributions. He was preparing to step down from the board.

Sensing that he was proud of his board membership, that he offered many qualities we needed from the board and that his time restrictions might last only a year or two longer, I offered to meet with him, in his office, at his convenience, before or after every board meeting. I kept him updated on activities and decisions of the board, and I kept him connected with the CEO and board leaders so that he could make contributions to board discussions outside of full board meetings. We tapped his expertise, but we also respected the restrictions on his time.

Responding to the customized engagement we offered, the donor in turn offered to travel to campus at other times on the condition that we should only ask him to make this trip when his presence was critically important. "If you need me once per year and I can possibly be there, I'll be there. If you need me a dozen times and I can do it, I'll be there. Waste my time once," he added, "and it will be the last time."

This donor remained engaged while we applied his valuable time and expertise in highly specific ways. He went on to make additional gifts that were among the largest in our organization's history. After a couple of years, his schedule became more flexible and he took a leadership position on the board.

Each prospective principal gift donor's combination of passion, experience, intellect, interest, available time and philanthropic objectives will be unique. Principal gift strategists must allocate resources such as people and time to respond in a customized way to each combination, in a way that will result in the deepest possible engagement of each prospective donor.

Be Careful About Applying Major Gift Strategies

Principal gift fundraising is not the same as major gift fundraising. Some of the same engagement strategies might work, but strategists must be careful about application of those strategies. The general rule of thumb is to customize after listening to the desires of each prospective donor. The following paragraphs provide a few examples.

Example one: galas. Many organizations rely on gala events to drive some or even a significant portion of fundraising revenue. In addition to producing revenue, galas allow organizations to showcase key people and accomplishments, provide a nice way for board members to introduce friends to the organization, and reinforce the commitment of donors by introducing them to like-minded people. Some donors love them; others dread them. Most people on an organization's top 40 list are active philanthropists, so a black-tie dinner is by no means something new.

Strategists should consider whether and how galas fit into customized engagement strategies. One principal gift donor might appreciate being asked to chair or co-chair an event rather than simply attend. Another might appreciate being honored and be happy, through the honor, to help the organization secure attendance of the donor's friends. Another might be grateful to know that their attendance is not required and that they're not going to be barraged with well-meaning gala chairs trying to persuade them to buy a table. Yet another might be thrilled to buy a table that the organization can use to invite others—like employees—who wouldn't otherwise be able to attend.

Example two: regional events. When an organization's principal curator, or music director or Nobel-prize-winning faculty member is traveling for the organization, prospective major gift donors might be invited to a special cocktail hour or dinner after the presentation. It might be more appropriate to ask a prospective principal gift donor whether they would prefer a private meeting in their home, or a small-group breakfast, or to be the one who introduces the featured speaker at the larger event. Depending on the number of donors in the area, this kind of customization may be possible for all prospective major gift donors, but chances are it will only be practical for one or two prospective donors, and those on the top 40 list should be considered first.

Time-Limited Engagement

Sometimes a short-term engagement—on a task force, or engaging a volunteer in one discussion or asking one favor, for example—can be more productive and more memorable for all concerned than service on a committee. Knowing they have contributed one essential piece of advice, opened one important door, or provided just the right venue for an event can make many volunteers feel much more valuable than sitting through hours of committee meetings. Task forces connected to specific strategic objectives help organizations refine plans and sharpen messages related to those plans; they simultaneously build ownership on the part of prospective donors for those objectives.

Service on a presidential search committee is another example of a time-limited, high-impact engagement. It also builds investment on the part of the donor in the success of the new president that can lead to gifts in support of the new leader's vision.

Time Is Often More Valuable Than Money

With every year that goes by, I understand more clearly why my older friends talk about time being more valuable than money—time with family, time with friends, time to focus on the people and activities we most love. Many high-net-worth donors, such as those serving in leadership positions in large companies, have intense pressures on their time. For them, time is more precious than money, regardless of their age.

Donors should not be asked to give time without a clear understanding—on the part of both organization and donor—of the amount of time needed and the expected return on investment of that time.

Older Prospective Donors

Most organizations will have multiple prospective donors older than 80 on their top 40 list. For some organizations, older prospective donors will comprise 50 percent or more of that list. Most deep engagement strategies, such as board and council membership, are not ideal for older donors. For example, many organizations have a mandatory retirement age for board members, and I've rarely seen that exceed 70 or 75 (this should be examined as people live and work longer). Also, as donors get older they are less and less likely to travel to an organization.

Organizations with older donors on the list need engagement strategies that take into account constraints as well as opportunities related to their age. Very often, this means going to the donor rather than having the donor come to the organization. Toward the beginning of my career, I visited with a woman who had given the largest gift ever received by my organization, a school of music. She was well into her 90s. She told me about how much she had loved to go to the opera, but that she was now limited to hearing opera on the radio. One of her greatest regrets, she said, was that she would never see in person "the nice young alumna of our school who is now having a big career at the Metropolitan Opera." I called that nice young woman, Renée Fleming—a superstar I never imagined I might meet—and asked her if she'd be willing to visit with the donor. We went together, and I listened to them talk for hours. It was one of the most magical afternoons of my life.

This leads to another aspect of engagement of older donors: stewardship of those with substantial bequest intentions. When a 68-year-old board member makes a large outright gift combined with a bequest, it may be 20 years before that board member dies, and possibly another 10 years before the board member's spouse dies. If no one from the organization has engaged that spouse, the expected bequest may never materialize. (See the essay on ultimate gifts in Appendix A for more on this subject.)

Keeping the Top 40 "Top of Mind"

In the chapter on identification, I talked about keeping donors "top of mind" for the CEO, board chair, development chair and chief development officer. Other members of the principal gift steering committee may also appropriately take on some responsibility for "top of mind" treatment.

By "top of mind," I mean that the CEO and others will be thinking about these prospective donors on a weekly basis. They will call a few of them when there is good news to share that is relevant to the interests of those donors. They will call them when there is bad news to share to make sure they hear it first from an organizational leader and get the facts. They will give them an opportunity to weigh in on plans in progress, or critical decisions, in ways that are appropriate to their interests and areas of expertise. They will consider them when making travel plans; even when there is not enough time to organize a donor event, there may be time to squeeze in a breakfast with one of those on the top 40 list. They will call or write to congratulate a top 40 prospective donor on the sale of a business, a promotion, a wedding or a child's graduation. They will recognize a birthday or anniversary when appropriate to the relationship.

They will also consult the top 40 list when it comes time to nominate new board members or form special task forces. They will consider expanding a special board committee, such as a presidential search committee or investment committee, to include a top 40 list member. They'll add them when appropriate to limited-space events, such as dinners with visiting dignitaries.

In short, they'll glance through the list at least weekly, send an email, pick up the phone, add someone to a list or otherwise make sure that no one on the top 40 list is overlooked when an appropriate opportunity for relationship-building presents itself.

To facilitate regular contact, the chief development officer will provide senior leaders and their executive assistants with regularly updated contact information and relevant dates for those on the top 40 list. This will include seasonal address changes and related dates, birthdates and other significant dates, such as when a donor is known to be planning to be on site for a performance, a reunion, a medical procedure and so on.

Rethinking "Moves Management"

A few years ago, at the "Inspiring the Largest Gifts of a Lifetime" CASE conference, my mentor and friend Dave Dunlop asked the participants, "How many of you have ever heard of moves management?" All hands in the room went up. "I was afraid of that," said Dave, who played a major role in creating and promoting the concept. He went on to explain that the *idea* of moves management is the right one; successful fundraising with major gift donors—individual and institutional—requires thoughtful planning for regular engagement. What Dave regrets is the name itself, especially the word "moves." He explained to the group that any suggestion of "putting the moves" on a prospective donor has no place in a culture of philanthropic partnership.

Fundraisers trained in moves management must rethink not only the name but also the implementation of moves-management approaches, especially with prospective principal gift donors. If fundraisers are truly partnership facilitators, then "prospect strategies" are more appropriately termed "partnership strategies." All of those involved in the partnership—including the donor—should help in shaping them.

Rather than sitting in an organization's conference room with colleagues and arguing about how and how often a donor should be engaged, facilitating fundraisers ask donors these questions and discuss their answers with colleagues. Facilitators ask donors how they want to be informed and how they want to be involved. They also inquire about how donors want to be asked, thanked and recognized.

Once donors are involved in shaping their own engagement strategies, there is no reason these strategies should not be visible to donors. Here are some examples of entries that might be found in partnership strategies shared with the donor:

- "Per Michele's wishes, work with her financial adviser, Anthony, to complete her $25,000 gift to the annual fund each year during the first week of December."
- "Work with Michele's assistant, Sandra, to schedule two lunches each year with the president so Michele can receive a personal report on the state of the organization, on the impact of her giving and on upcoming initiatives that might be of greatest interest to her. Be sure the report on the professorship she endowed is sent in advance of the fall lunch, as she likes to discuss this report with the president."
- "Be sure that the board chair or nominating committee chair checks in with Michele at least once a year on the idea of board membership. Michele has stated that she is not yet ready to join the board, but that she may be ready in the next few years."
- "Invite Michele to events in the Distinguished Speakers Series, including special dinners with the speakers. She loves this series and, though business travel often prevents her from attending, she likes to be kept aware and included. When there are speakers focusing on the arts, she would especially like to know well in advance and will do her best to plan her schedule around these. Keep Sandra in this loop as well."
- "Assist Michele as she builds on the important investments she has made in the arts (her personal passion) and in mechanical engineering (where she endowed the professorship in memory of her father). As appropriate, schedule meetings with the arts dean, the music department chair, the engineering dean and the mechanical engineering department chair. She likes the professor who holds her chair, and she would like to have a chance to meet with him on occasion as well, though it need not be every year. Keep her informed of major events, accomplishments, challenges and changes in these two areas. Invite

her into discussions about new initiatives, as early in the process as feasible. She would like to support new initiatives, but she'd also like to assist in strategizing about how to engage the interest of others."

- "With the new campaign coming, discuss ways Michele might like to be involved, and continue discussing the importance of her making a leadership gift early in the campaign."

Before partnerships are fully developed, partnership strategies may be less ready for sharing with prospective donors. The facilitator's objective, however, should be to move toward engagement strategies that are informed by donors and could easily be shared with them at any time. Applying such a test ("Would I be willing to share this partnership strategy with the donor?") helps fundraisers avoid "putting the moves" on donors and succeed instead in building long-term, authentic partnerships.

Summary

Successful engagement strategies for prospective principal gift donors are as unique as the donors themselves. They are informed by donor interests and objectives, and they are customized. Above all, prospective principal gift donors are top of mind for senior leaders—members of the top 40 list get as much mindshare as any other senior organizational leader. They are partners in shaping their engagement strategies, and they view themselves and are viewed as essential partners in creating the organization's future.

Chapter 7

AUTHENTICITY

When I discuss the character of fundraisers with donors and organizational leaders, one quality consistently emerges as critical to success as well as happiness: authenticity.

In all fundraising, and especially in principal gift fundraising, it is not enough to represent a worthy organization. Fundraisers—everyone involved in the principal gift fundraising process—must gain and sustain the belief and confidence of colleagues and potential donors. For belief and confidence to be strong, fundraisers must have genuine commitment to the organizations they are serving, an earnest desire to help generous people make successful and satisfying gifts, and authenticity in all interactions.

Genuine Commitment to the Organization

"The best nonprofit managers and staff members I've known have a deep, personal connection with an organization's mission," says Joan Harris, a generous donor and experienced board leader who supports organizations in Chicago, Aspen, New York, and elsewhere. "They relate, intimately, to the passion of board members, volunteers, and donors, and this results in much more effective fundraising."

Fundraisers must be knowledgeable about what their organizations want to do and honest about what those organizations are able to do. A personal commitment to the organization and its mission is a big plus, as Joan notes above. At the very least, a professional commitment must be informed through careful study and engagement with organizational leaders. Fundraisers must also know and be transparent about an organization's capability to follow through on all promises made to donors.

A Desire To Help Generous People Make Successful and Satisfying Gifts

The 2016 U.S. Trust Study of High Net Worth Philanthropy found that, "When determining which causes or nonprofit organizations to support financially, the majority of HNW [defined in the study as net worth of $1 million or more excluding a primary home] individuals draw upon their personal values (78 percent) ...." Only 6.4 percent cited a "compelling pitch" as a contributing factor (U.S. Trust and IUPUI 2016).

Fundraisers must be prepared to represent an organization professionally, knowledgeably and passionately. They must be equally prepared to learn the values, hopes, dreams and motivations of donors. A good rule of thumb for fundraisers is "two ears, one mouth"—they should listen twice as much as they talk.

Notice that I do not say "earnest desire to help generous people make large gifts *to a specific organization*." That may happen—indeed it must happen for organizations to thrive and for professional fundraisers to keep their jobs! Starting with a narrow focus on securing a gift from a donor to a specific organization, however, diminishes effectiveness of fundraisers and reduces the likelihood of establishing trust.

Fundraisers should begin, instead, with a desire to learn the overall philanthropic objectives of prospective donors, as discussed in Chapter 1. Only by listening to donors can fundraisers tap into the full potential of what each donor and their organization might accomplish together. Starting with organizational needs almost always narrows the scope of the conversation and thus the size of a potential gift.

Beyond simply asking how a potential donor is doing, an excellent opening question for fundraisers is, "What are you trying to accomplish with your philanthropy—what impact would you like to have—and how might I help?" There is a critical difference between asking about a donor's philanthropic objectives within the constraints of an organization's objectives and asking about those philanthropic objectives even before getting to the specifics of an organization's plans. Still, in talking and working with hundreds of leading philanthropists over the years, I've come to learn that they are rarely, if ever, asked about their overall philanthropic objectives. Most reported that they've never been asked. Indeed, I have never been asked, even though I have given to many organizations. Even if fundraisers are prepared to listen to donors, they miss out on a great deal of information if they start by talking only about their own organizations and what donors are thinking only in the context of those organizations. Such conversations lead to the development of unidimensional relationships—not truly authentic relationships.

Fundraisers must also listen to donors' motivations in giving—intellectual as well as psychological. The philanthropic process is often personal and emotional. Decisions about giving affect family wealth and inheritances. Gifts are sometimes in response to joyful experiences, such as a graduation, a wedding or a successful medical treatment. They are sometimes in response to a painful experience—the death of a loved one, or being the victim of discrimination. They are sometimes prompted by religious conviction, other times by gratitude and still other times by a deep concern about a societal problem.

Some donors will want to make a highly visible gift, often to encourage others to follow their example. Others will want to keep a gift very private, for a wide variety of reasons. I worked with one donor, for example, who was concerned that making a large gift would put his children at risk of kidnapping, since the extent of his wealth would be made much more public.

In short, fundraisers should begin relationships with generous people by asking them what they are trying to accomplish. Then they need to listen carefully and demonstrate genuine desire and intent to help the donors. In doing so, fundraisers will help donors give in effective as well as satisfying ways, leading to larger gifts for their organizations and for society overall.

Authenticity in All Interactions

Building relationships involves finding points of connection. Some of those will be points of connection between the donor's passions and the organization's strategic plans. Some will be points of connection between the donor and people leading and doing the work of the organization, possibly including the fundraiser assigned to the donor. By listening, fundraisers help establish and support authentic relationships built on mutual respect and trust.

Donors want to talk to real people—people who listen, sympathize, empathize and genuinely want donors to succeed in helping the organizations they are supporting and helping society as a result. One valued colleague shared some advice for fundraisers that has been very important in her career: "Be an interesting, interested person, so that other interesting, interested people will want to talk to you." Donors don't want to hear "institution speak" or sales pitches. They would rather see passion and integrity, even if that sometimes means seeing flaws. Fundraisers should be knowledgeable and prepared, but an over-rehearsed presentation can easily come across as inauthentic.

Fundraisers must not insult donor intelligence or condescend by avoiding complicated or controversial topics. They don't need to air dirty laundry unnecessarily, but if donors are aware of disagreement among key leaders on how to proceed, glossing over internal challenges will only diminish confidence in fundraisers and their organizations. Donors may agree with planning related to a gift under discussion but disagree with some other organizational decision. It is important to be as candid as possible. Donors are much more likely to overcome frustration with a particular decision when fundraisers share the process leaders went through to weigh the pros and cons. Donors know perfectly well that organizations aren't perfect, and they know they won't always agree with every leader's thinking. They will trust fundraisers much more if these professionals are honest, even as they cast decisions and opportunities in the best possible light. Above all, fundraisers must never resort to dishonesty to get a gift.

Potential donors who have felt ignored or marginalized by an organization likely will be more skeptical about the readiness and willingness of organizational representatives to listen to their concerns and their philanthropic objectives. Those who have experienced inauthenticity in the past will have heightened sensitivity and will immediately detect inauthentic remarks or behavior. Fundraisers must be prepared for active listening and ready to invest time and care in establishing a relationship that is authentic and that potential donors experience as authentic, before jumping into gift conversations.

Differences in gender, race, ethnicity, sexual orientation, nationality, language or age can introduce additional obstacles to effective communication and lead to inauthenticity or the perception of inauthenticity. An authentic shared passion for an organization helps establish common ground. Careful thought about who to involve in relationship building—for example, introducing others into the process with multiple points of connection—may allow for yet more authentic communication early in the relationship.

Sometimes Authenticity Means Saying "No"

Authenticity means that sometimes fundraisers must say "no," and they need the courage, conviction and support to do so. Occasionally, a donor will try to take advantage or offer a gift inconsistent with an organization's mission or capabilities. In such cases the answer must be "no." Occasionally, a boss will push a fundraiser to ask for the wrong gift at the wrong time. There, too, the fundraiser may have to find a way to say "no." Sometimes fundraisers must say "no" simply to be honest partners, so that colleagues and donors will trust them the next time.

As partners, however, "no" is rarely the appropriate full answer. When I've said "no" to a donor, it is almost always because I believe the donor's gift would not succeed—that they would not be proud of the result. "No, period," can be a fundraiser's answer when their organization does not want restrictions donors may want to impose upon gifts, but a more nuanced tack would be more productive. In such cases I would advise saying something along these lines: "I know what the organization is trying to accomplish, and I know what you are aiming to accomplish with your philanthropy, and I'd like to explain to you why this gift will not be successful in our organization—or for you—at this moment in time." That nuanced version of "no" requires knowledge of organizational objectives and capacity as well as knowledge of donor objectives. Indeed, an informed response of "no" in the context of a culture of philanthropic partnership requires that fundraisers have acquired both types of knowledge.

One further point in this regard: If fundraisers can help donors by introducing them to other institutions that are better positioned to make their giving successful, they should consider doing so. Knowing that fundraisers have listened to them and are serious about helping them give wisely, those donors will be much more likely to come back for further conversation and advice about future gifts.

Navigating Tricky Waters with Authenticity

Because of the personal motivations involved in giving, discussions with donors can wander into a variety of highly personal areas, including race, gender, sexual orientation, family dynamics, politics and religion. Donors may raise such issues when talking about a gift, or simply when they are getting to know an organizational representative. It is only natural that donors will occasionally express opinions and reveal prejudices that an organizational representative may not share.

Some fundraising consultants suggest that fundraisers should avoid such discussions and steer the conversation away from anything not specifically related to a gift proposal. Most successful fundraisers I know are quick to disagree, and vehemently. The life experiences of a donor have significant bearing on their personal decisions, and their giving decisions, as stated above, are often highly personal. Religious beliefs and family history and dynamics often play a significant role in a donor's life and sometimes have a direct bearing on considerations of a specific gift. All our experiences—good and bad—shape who we are and the values that consciously and unconsciously inform giving decisions.

Early in my fundraising career, one of my most important mentors, Dave Dunlop, told me that I would undoubtedly find myself from time to time in uncomfortable situations, with donors making political statements with which I disagreed, making discriminatory comments that offended me or otherwise demonstrating beliefs that ran counter to mine or those held by leaders in my organization. He gave important counsel on how to react and respond, but he began with a simple but powerful statement that every manager of fundraisers should consider as they mentor others: "Use your best judgment, and know that I will back you up."

As a new fundraiser, I was terrified. I wondered whether I had chosen the right career path. Before too long, I heard racial slurs, misogynistic comments, hateful observations about one of my organization's leaders and political remarks that made me shudder. As I compared notes with colleagues, I found that they, too, had been placed in challenging situations. African-American colleagues had doors slammed in their faces. Gay colleagues were forced to listen to homophobic rants. Several colleagues—men as well as women—experienced subtle and not-so-subtle sexual advances from potential donors. Many learned things about a donor's family dynamics they would rather not know.

How should fundraisers respond? Should they argue? Leave? Change the subject? To what degree should they share their own feelings or speak up when they're offended? Should they laugh along with the offensive joke, or murmur something non-committal and try to move the conversation along?

Do they reveal that they're Jewish, or gay, or that their spouse is a person of a different race or nationality? Do they offer a political opinion when the donor asks for one? Do they argue when the donor says their organization's president is steering the ship in the wrong direction? Do they go along to get along?

Further, does the answer to these questions change if the gift under discussion is $1 million? When the gift represents 25 percent of the entire fiscal year's fundraising goal? When all the senior people in the fundraiser's organization are desperately hoping the gift will become a reality?

After thirty years in the field, the only thing that is clear is that there is no one right answer to how fundraisers should respond. The best advice I have heard, and the best advice I can give, is that fundraisers should focus on the principal purposes of their fundraising meetings. Getting back to the point of the meeting is usually an effective way to steer clear of an unproductive argument. In challenging conversations, fundraisers must remember that they are representatives of their organizations and then exercise sound judgment. Ideally, they will do so knowing that their organizational colleagues will support them even when they make mistakes.

A colleague shared this relevant story: "I met during the heat of a recent election with one of our top donors. We couldn't possibly be further apart politically. She acknowledged that difference early in our conversation, saying to me, 'I know we have complete disagreement on political issues but we also care a lot about this organization, and that's what we're doing together.' It completely removed the elephant—or donkey—in the room and let us get on with a very pleasant conversation about her giving plans."

Sometimes, donors or other people in powerful positions abuse that power. Fundraisers must never be made to feel that such an abuse must be overlooked, even if they decide not to challenge it in the moment. Chief development officers and other supervisors should encourage open dialogue so that fundraisers feel safe in raising concerns and so that such abuses can be addressed appropriately.

Donors have flaws, and so do those who are helping to facilitate their giving. But the fundraising profession is rooted in optimism—fundraisers look for the best in people and organizations. Accordingly, I would suggest that nonprofit leaders need to trust that colleagues and donors, like family and friends, will sort out any differences they might have and find each other worthy partners in accomplishing shared aspirations. If donors and fundraisers look for the best in each other and trust that they are each using their best judgment, they have the basis for a lasting, productive relationship. Fundraisers must be alert to their own personal biases and frustrations, to be sure, and would do well always to remember that they are stewards of their organizations' values and reputations. But they should also be themselves, and let donors be themselves, giving everyone the best chance at an authentic, open dialogue aimed at helping donors and organizations accomplish wonderful things, together.

One final note on this topic: The more personally fundraisers are invested in the missions of their organizations, the easier it is for them to be authentic and the more likely that they and donors will find significant common ground. Conversely, if fundraisers' values are not closely aligned with the values of the organizations they are serving, chances are that their values will also not be aligned with the values of their organizations' donors.

Friendships Sometimes Emerge

I have heard fundraising consultants suggest that fundraisers must never allow relationships with donors to develop into friendships. Nonsense! Every leading philanthropist I know counts nonprofit leaders, including fundraising professionals, among their friends. And every successful fundraiser I know has developed a handful of enduring friendships with philanthropists.

At the same time, friendship is not and cannot be the main objective of the fundraiser-donor relationship. In fact, I would go further to say that even the *professional* relationship between fundraiser and donor cannot be the primary relationship objective—the principal relationship should be between donor and organization. That is accomplished only when the fundraiser removes self and ego and ensures that the donor develops strong and lasting relationships with many organizational representatives who are in a position to facilitate successful philanthropic investments on the part of the donor.

If priorities are right, and friendship is not the objective, the friendships between donors and fundraisers that occasionally emerge should not be discouraged. It is inevitable that friendships will sometimes spring naturally from an authentic, long-term fundraiser-donor relationship. In some situations, avoiding a natural friendship would be inauthentic and damaging.

I once worked with a donor couple, a man and woman who were both in their late 80s. We worked together for several years. At one point, I scheduled a visit and learned that I would be there the same week that the man was turning 90. They were celebrating alone and had no remaining family and very few living friends, none of whom lived nearby. Knowing how difficult it was for them to go out or cook for themselves, I offered to make a birthday dinner in their home. They were thrilled.

I visited that couple once or twice each year. About five years after the birthday evening, I called to schedule a visit and learned that the husband had died. His widow asked if I could take her to the funeral home to pick up his ashes because she had no other way of getting there. It didn't occur to me to tell her this might be stepping over a line from professional duties to personal. I said "yes" without hesitation.

By contrast, a friend and leading philanthropist shared a story of joining a board, knowing she and her husband would be asked for a large gift. In the months following her decision to join the board, she and her husband went out to dinner several times with another board member and his wife and attended a couple of performances together. They had a wonderful time and enjoyed what my friend considered to be an emerging, close friendship. After a year, the other board member asked my friend and her husband for a substantial gift, as expected, and they happily agreed. My friend never heard again from the other couple, socially. "It was all cultivation," she told me. The organization received the gift, but my friend was deeply hurt by the experience. While her relationship with the organization remained strong, thanks to relationships with other board members and senior staff, this lack of authenticity could easily have created lasting damage. She shared the story hoping that it would encourage other fundraisers—professional and volunteer—to avoid such behavior.

Authenticity and Happiness

I have discussed how important authenticity is to success in the fundraising profession, and success certainly contributes to happiness. Even when fundraising is not successful per se, authenticity in fundraising can still lead to happiness. If fundraisers raise money for organizations about which they are personally passionate, they will experience the advancement of those organizations as much more than just a professional accomplishment. And when they help generous people make gifts with impact and gifts that the donors find satisfying, the happiness they give the donors will spill over, giving the fundraisers much more satisfaction than any promotion or raise ever will. For me, nothing beats the moments when I have seen donors shed tears of joy after making a gift. These have been among the happiest moments of my life.

Appendix A

ULTIMATE GIFTS AND THE BABY BOOM

When I was writing this book, I asked Robert Sharpe, a leading authority on gift planning and a friend and colleague of many years, to share his insights about the largest gifts donors will make in their lifetimes and through their estates—their ultimate gifts. His essay complements and provides additional context for the thoughts I have shared in this book, and I am delighted to include his perspectives.

—Ronald J. Schiller

Ultimate Gifts and the Baby Boom
By Robert F. Sharpe Jr.

When I first began my career in nonprofit development, like many others I encountered a bewildering array of terms that purported to describe different types of gifts. These included the terms "annual gifts," "major gifts," "deferred gifts," "endowment gifts," "capital gifts," "leadership gifts," "legacy gifts," "membership gifts," direct-mail gifts" and "planned gifts." I also discovered that in many organizations, especially larger ones, there would be one or more people with the title "Director of…" for each of these "types" of gifts.

The more I thought about it the more I realized these were not types of gifts at all. Rather, they were labels that had been placed on gifts based on different criteria, such as timing (annual, deferred), the size of the gift (major, leadership, principal), the use of the funds (endowment, capital), the way the gift was raised (membership, direct mail) or the way the gift was structured (planned).

Over the years, I became more and more convinced that these misappellations and the organizational silos they spawned and came to describe were at the root of much of the failure or under-performance of fundraising initiatives. The larger and more "sophisticated" the program, the more that seemed to be true. I also realized that those organizations that operated under a different rubric seemed to thrive despite economic, demographic and other challenges.

In the mid-1990s, David Dunlop—a professional colleague and highly respected leader in principal gifts—and I decided to structure a conference for CASE entitled "Inspiring the Largest Gift of a Lifetime." Ron Schiller, among others mentored by Dave, has also been an integral part of the faculty over the years. The purpose of this conference, now having been attended by more than 2,000 fundraisers, was to break down destructive barriers to effective fundraising through a different approach that considered the process of giving from the perspective of the *donor*, rather than through the lens of institutional needs and timing.

Building on what he had learned over his many years of experience, Dave concluded that from the donor's perspective there were only three types of gifts. He referred to these categories of gifts as "regular," "special" and "ultimate."

In this essay, my goal is to describe why understanding Dave's concept of "ultimate" gift is central to success in efforts to encourage the largest gifts. I will also discuss the importance of paying attention to the baby-boom generation, since baby boomers will make most of the largest gifts received by organizations for the next several decades.

"Regular" and "Special" Gifts

Before defining and discussing "ultimate" gifts, I first want to describe the other two types of gifts, for context.

A "regular" gift is a gift that is made on a periodic basis: in some cases once a year, in others once a month, and still others on a weekly basis. These gifts are usually a relatively small amount given from a donor's income. The donor typically sets the amount with the knowledge and anticipation that the gift will be expected to be repeated over time. Efforts to encourage regular gifts come in the form of annual giving programs, membership programs, sponsorship efforts, periodic mass mailings and online solicitations designed to acquire as many donors as possible. Donors of larger regular gifts are sometimes referred to as "major donors," "leadership donors" or other terms designed to set them apart for the purposes of stewardship of their giving and their relationship with the organization.

Regular gift fundraising may be described as *speculative* in nature. Much of the fundraising activity of the organization is devoted to asking for funds with not a great deal of attention paid to building personal relationships with the masses of donors of smaller amounts. These gifts are normally in the form of cash, check or a credit card payment and represent a small portion of a donor's cash or liquid assets.

Many organizations and institutions never move beyond regular gift fundraising. As a result, they live a hand-to-mouth existence with few, if any, reserves or endowment funds.

The second type of gift in the Dunlop lexicon is the "special" gift. These gifts are described as special because they often come from donors who are already making regular gifts. Special gifts are gifts made in what historically have been known as capital campaigns. That is because special gift efforts are undertaken when a nonprofit organization finds itself in need of capital for buildings or other substantial undertakings that cannot be financed from regular giving or debt.

Special gifts are usually 10, 20, even 100 or more times the size of regular gifts. Special gifts have historically been raised primarily through campaigns designed to convince regular and, in some cases, first–time donors to give larger amounts. These gifts are normally restricted to a project or projects that drove the need for a campaign in the first place. Special gifts are sometimes among the largest gifts an organization receives in any given year.

The larger a special gift, the more likely it is to be made in a form other than cash. That is because wealthy individuals do not normally become wealthy or build their wealth by keeping all their assets in checking accounts. For this and other reasons, special gift efforts have traditionally been undertaken by organizations with significant staff or other resources available to them for facilitating noncash gifts. That is changing with the democratization of special gift efforts through the rise of donor–advised funds and other services provided by both for–profit and nonprofit entities devoted to helping organizations facilitate special gifts funded with assets other than cash.

While most building and other capital needs historically have been met through efforts to encourage special gifts, it is rare to see significant amounts of reserve funds or unrestricted endowment funds raised through special gifts. Endowments that are restricted to scholarship funds, chairs, research funds, advocacy funds and so on—needs that can be transformed into a *thing*—can be named and thus take on more urgency or meaning to a donor. Few donors are willing to make special gifts from their capital resources to be held in an unrestricted way that may or may not be spent by unknown future leaders on unknown future needs.

Efforts to raise special gifts are normally more *transactional* in nature. Through naming opportunities and other similar enticements, some donors are persuaded to make significant capital gifts out of motivations that may include the desire to memorialize themselves, their loved ones or others. Most buildings or restricted funds of consequence bear the name of a donor. Anonymous gifts to campaigns are relatively rare.

Because of their transactional nature and the temptation to "sell" naming and other recognition to donors, special-gift development efforts often take on many of the characteristics of sales activity that is common in the for-profit world. Sales terminology such as "prospects," "leads" and "closing" (as in "closing a gift") have become a part of the vocabulary of many staff members and volunteers engaged in this type of fundraising.

Ultimate Gifts Defined

It is only with an understanding of regular and special gifts that one can fully understand what sets the "ultimate" gift apart.

Some have come to define "ultimate" gift by size alone. While definitions tied to the size of a gift are on the right track, they miss the mark. Ultimate gifts are not defined by what is considered a large gift by an organization but rather *by the size of the gift in relation to both the capacity and level of commitment of a donor*. In other words, while some ultimate gifts will be among the largest gifts an organization receives, all will be the largest gifts donors make.

Some fundraisers define "ultimate" gift according to timing. An ultimate gift may be the final gift of a donor, made through an estate, but it might also be made earlier in life, with only small gifts to follow, and perhaps without any gift made in the estate. This definition of ultimate as "final," associated with timing, also misses the mark of the Dunlop concept.

I define the ultimate gift as follows: "The ultimate gift is the largest gift a donor is capable of forming the intent to make in support of a particular charitable interest." This definition encompasses several meanings of ultimate—largest, best, most expressive of the donor's motivation and final—and can involve any combination of these.

While ultimate gifts can sometimes be the first gift a donor makes, they are usually only made after a significant period of engagement with the organization supported by several of the organization's representatives. The donor will usually have personal relationships with professors, counselors, clergy, researchers, physicians, artists and other program-side team members as well as with volunteers, development staff members and other members of senior management, past and present.

Timing of Ultimate Gifts

Most experienced fundraisers can recall cases where a wealthy, highly committed donor has made very large outright gifts during their lifetime and then no estate gift. Staff and volunteer leadership may have assumed that the organization would receive large distributions upon the longtime donor's passing. Many donors will decide to make their ultimate gift during their lifetimes and as a result will give nothing further through their estate.

At the same time, many fundraisers can recall numerous instances when a relatively large bequest was received through a donor's estate, despite a long history of unremarkable regular gifts and no history of special gifts to capital campaigns. In many cases, these "surprise" bequests constitute what was the donor's ultimate gift.

For many donors, an ultimate gift is of a magnitude that will only be completed through an estate. The financial realities that rule the economic life of all but the very wealthy too often preclude the completion of the ultimate gift during life. The fear of dying before fulfilling financial obligations to children and others, the concern that one may outlive resources later in life, and worries about disability or other economic emergencies are powerful enough to overwhelm even the strongest intent, even when it appears that a donor enjoys a substantial capacity to give.

Restriction of Ultimate Gifts

Ultimate gifts completed during a donor's lifetime are very likely to be restricted to a use that is rooted in the donor's motivation for the gift. In contrast, ultimate gifts received through an unremarkable lifetime donor's estate are normally not heavily restricted, if at all. This is because when the donor includes such a gift in an estate plan they are normally not aware of when their demise will trigger the gift. Such donors are often thoughtful people who refrain from restricting gifts to purposes that may no longer be a priority at the time of their death.

History reveals that many of the largest unrestricted endowments are the result of estates gifts from donors who left unrestricted bequests that were subsequently restricted by boards to reserves or quasi-endowment (board-restricted endowment funds) that could be used as ongoing needs required.

Encouraging Ultimate Gifts

Many nonprofit organizations, especially those with robust major gift programs, are aware of donors capable of making their ultimate gift during their lifetime and actively pursue multi-faceted efforts to assist donors in the process of determining the best time during their lifetime to make that gift. While such efforts may yield quick results, a more typical pattern for seeing a lifetime ultimate gift through to completion is that they take years to nurture and depend on work by several generations of development officers.

It is rare to be informed in advance of more than 25 percent of gifts received through estates, including those that amount to a donor's ultimate gift. Some fundraisers find that advanced notification occurs in as few as one in 15 to 20 estates. How, then, do fundraisers encourage ultimate gifts that are received through estates but are unknown prior to the passing of the donor? Many of these will be ultimate gifts for the donor, and some will be among an organization's largest gifts in a given year. Indeed, they may perhaps count among the largest gifts the organization has ever received.

The first step is to establish and sustain a culture that celebrates philanthropic partnership, in which all donors develop ownership of an organization and its future. In such cultures, donors are considered insiders, not outsiders. When they include an organization in their final will, they have elevated it to a status akin to that of family member.

It is therefore essential to understand the profile of donors who have made ultimate gifts through bequests to an organization and make sure that the organization is well positioned in the minds of donors of a similar profile. Such a profile may suggest the establishment of recognition programs based on longevity of giving and cumulative giving in addition to the more common programs that recognize donors based on size of their regular or special gifts. A special thank you to a 35-year-long donor with recognition of their longevity of giving may go a long way when that donor is asked by an attorney, when preparing a final will (the only will that matters), if their charitable interests have changed since they made an earlier will. The same is true when a donor of 50 gifts of $50 is recognized as a $2,500 cumulative donor.

Why engage in these efforts? Not all long-term donors will make their ultimate gift through an estate, but many of the ones who *do* take that step will be those who feel deep affiliation with the organization to the end of their lives. Recognition of longevity of giving and cumulative giving regardless of size of gifts increases the likelihood of continued giving, even at modest amounts, and this in turn increases the likelihood of commitment that is sustained through to the last will.

Ongoing stewardship of those who reveal their estate gift intentions in advance is also critically important. Many organizations that have discovered bequests during capital campaigns have unfortunately been removed from a number of those estate plans due to lack of sustained stewardship. In my experience, the younger donors are when they reveal their intentions, the more likely that their expected gifts will not be received when they die. Many will have gone through multiple revisions of their wills by that time, and memories of earlier commitments may be distant or even unpleasant in the cases of organizations that have provided little to no proper stewardship.

While it is impossible to devise a one-size-fits-all approach to maintaining these relationships, one simple comparison can be a good guide in this process. Fundraisers should ask themselves: "What if my aunt called and told me she had included me in her will? What would I do next? Ask for documentation? Ask how much I can expect to receive?" Most would not take that approach, of course, and would simply say "thank you." What would happen if the fundraiser's aunt was ignored for the rest of her life? When donors reveal estate plans, they are revealing deeply personal intentions, and fundraisers should be very careful about how they respond and how they steward these generous individuals.

Everything would change, however, if the aunt wanted to move into the fundraiser's home and have the fundraiser care for her for the rest of her life in exchange for a bequest. That is a *transaction* and should be treated as such. The same is true if a donor is requesting that a building or program be named in exchange for a bequest. An organization won't necessarily reject the request, but documentation such as additional gift agreements will be needed.

While each donor is different, a common denominator is that the only entities found in wills are close family, close friends and nonprofit organizations. A donor who has made a bequest intention is treating the recipient organization like a family member, and the organizational representative would do well to treat that donor with reciprocity, guided by thinking about that generous aunt.

Accelerated Ultimate Gifts

Donors who include ultimate gifts in their estates when they are younger, say in their 60s or 70s, may find their life circumstances to be very different when they are in their 80s or 90s. They may be widowed and no longer concerned about a surviving spouse; their children and grandchildren may now be educated and on their own; they may have decided that they will not likely outlive their resources, and they may, in fact, have more wealth than they did 20 years earlier when they made their bequest commitment. Donors may also come to realize that they are nearing the end of life and may like to see gifts come to fruition during their lifetimes.

Donors who have been well-stewarded in their later years may decide to *accelerate* a bequest and complete a gift prior to death. Learning to listen to older donors and pick up on clues that they may be thinking in these terms will increasingly be important skills for those charged with fundraising responsibilities. Many bequests that are accelerated late in a donor's life will be large, as they stem from a lifetime of earning and saving. Some of these accelerated bequests will be among an organization's largest gifts.

Further Thoughts on Timing

It is rare that a donor will make a regular, special and ultimate-gift commitment in one day, one month, one year or even one decade. The chart on the following page summarizes the typical timing of types of gifts donors make.

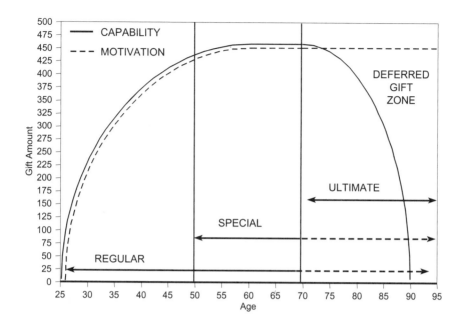

Knowing where a donor falls in this life cycle is critical to knowing when to encourage which type of gift. Few younger donors will make special or ultimate gifts. Middle-age donors may make both regular and special gifts but have not typically reached a point in life where they are in touch with their priorities to the point of deciding ultimate gifts. Older donors can in some cases be making regular gifts, special gifts and planning for or making their ultimate gifts—all at the same time.

The Baby Boom and Ultimate Giving

With the passing of members of the G.I. generation and the cohort that followed, the silent generation, we are now seeing the leading edge of the baby-boom generation move into the phase of life where most will make their largest gift of a lifetime. The oldest baby boomers turned 70 in 2016. With fewer donors coming behind them, due to decreased birth rates after the boom, it is critical that fundraisers be prepared to assist this group of individuals. As they move into the final phase of their lives, members of the generation that has in many ways defined the last 50 years will be prepared and driven to transform the future through their current and deferred ultimate gifts.

Year after year, the majority of the top 50 gifts in America have come from donors age 70 and older. For the next several decades, most of the largest gifts will come from baby boomers who have reached this age milestone. When selecting prospective principal gift donors, organizational leaders must consider all potential corporate, foundation, and individual donors, using the criteria that Ron Schiller outlines in this book, including capacity, inclination and philanthropic priority. Fundraisers can and should expect, however, to find much of the greatest capacity and readiness among a growing number of individuals and families in the ultimate giving zone—those who have passed the age of 70.

Appendix B

A JOYFUL CAREER IN PHILANTHROPY

When asked to share my own thoughts on sustaining joy in this profession, my first response is, "Don't chase wealthy people; enable philanthropy." That message is so fundamental that I made it the focus of the first chapter in this book. As simple as that principle is, however, I have seen it overlooked by many colleagues. Many suffer needlessly as they fret about how to separate a wealthy person from her money, and many ultimately drop out of the profession entirely. I have also observed that too many development professionals do far too little to nurture relationships with those who have already expressed, sometimes repeatedly, their desire to help an organization. With that in mind, my second and closely related piece of advice is, "If you're feeling frustrated, get out of your office and visit a donor."

As I prepared to write this book, I asked colleagues with 25 or more years of experience in development and advancement and significant success in principal gift fundraising to share their own thoughts on sustaining a joyful career in philanthropy. They have facilitated large gifts for arts organizations, colleges and universities, medical centers and other organizations across the country. While the comments here are offered without attribution, the names of the colleagues who offered their thoughts are included in this book's acknowledgments.

—Ronald J. Schiller

WORDS OF WISDOM
A Collection of Thoughts from Colleagues in Development and Advancement

Reflections on What Has Brought Joy as a Professional Fundraiser

- The people! The donors, and colleagues focused on helping philanthropists and organizations achieve great things together. (Almost everyone who contributed put this as No. 1 on their lists.) One contributor noted, "Most days are great, but when things get squirrely, the best way back to true north is to get with good people—your dearest and most trusted donors and colleagues, who remind us why we do this work."

- The relationships. "We get to build relationships with exceptional people. Many are relationships that last a lifetime."

- Helping people help others; facilitating philanthropy.

- The ability to connect like-minded people, build understanding and transform organizations.

- Getting to see and experience firsthand the impact of the gifts we help facilitate.

- Hearing donors express the happiness they've experienced in making a gift. "I heard one donor say, 'This gift has transformed my life.'"

- Being surrounded by brilliant and motivated people striving to do better and be better.

- Sharing and celebrating success with others. "Development is a team sport."

- Watching former staff members and other colleagues become successful leaders in the profession.

- "One of my colleagues is an experimental psychologist whose work focuses on the impact of giving and volunteering; indications are that positive impact extends to physiological benefits. This understanding will give all of us yet another reason to derive joy from our work."

- "I am privileged to work with the better angels of human nature. What our donors and institutional leaders do literally touches and shapes the ages. What's not to like?"

Words of Wisdom for Current and Aspiring Development Professionals and Volunteers

- Work in support of a cause or institution you believe in. "If you wouldn't be a donor or volunteer yourself, think carefully about whether you're working for the right organization."

- Spend time with donors and with people most affected by the gifts your organization receives. Both remind us, directly and on a very personal level, why we do what we do.

- Remain donor-centered, helping donors share the contagious thrill of making a difference.

- Fundraising is teaching people the joy of giving. Work with your team and with other donors to introduce first-time donors to that satisfaction and joy.

- Get to know joyful givers—their joy will add to your own.

- Be discerning about the people you work with every day. Much of your joy will come from being part of a team that enables you to accomplish more than you could ever accomplish on your own.

- If you are a chief development officer, accept responsibility for having the right mix of people, with the right skill sets, and with shared values that fit the organization, in the proper roles. Your team's morale, and ability of team members to derive joy in their work, depends on careful hiring and on dealing with personnel problems quickly, discreetly and decisively. "I've rarely regretted asking someone to leave too quickly; I've often regretted waiting too long to remove a negative influence on the team."

- Be smart about the egos and politics that inevitably surround you— don't get immersed in them.

- To win wars, you don't have to win all the battles.

- Have a kind and forgiving nature.

- Keep a long view. Working with donors over the course of years, even decades, allows you to see them mature in their philanthropy and deepen their own sense of satisfaction and joy.

- Find a niche that best suits your temperament, instead of trying to climb a career ladder. Stick with what you're good at, and what you love, and make that your specialty.

- Take advantage of professional networking opportunities, and invest time and care in the professional and personal relationships that emerge.

- Be loyal and committed to the people and institutions you serve.

- Avoid expressing negative opinions of others.

- Focus on solutions rather than problems. Be a problem solver.

- Give back to the profession, teaching new development and advancement professionals about the challenges and opportunities—and joy—of a career in philanthropy.

In closing, a story from my Aspen Leadership Group colleague and former principal gift fundraiser, Tim Child: "A donor once told me the story of a president of a small cultural organization visiting along with his development director. The organization had given this donor and his family many wonderful experiences over many years. When the president finally summoned the courage to ask for a gift, the request was relatively small. The donor excused himself, went to his office, and returned with a check for $1 million. In telling me the story, the donor's face absolutely lit up, in part because he had a mischievous sense of humor, in part because he cherished the memory of the shocked president rendered speechless, and most of all because the act of giving for him and his wife was an utterly joyous experience."

PRINCIPAL GIFTS CHECKLIST

Markers of a Program in Which the Ten Top Gifts are as Large as Possible for that Organization

Culture

☐ Organizational leaders embrace top donors as partners in creating the organization's future, not as outsiders.

☐ Fundraisers view their role as that of facilitator more than solicitor.

☐ Donors, organizational leaders, and staff members and volunteers involved in fundraising have high levels of belief and confidence in the organization, its leaders and its plans.

Identification

☐ The organization has identified 40 prospective donors with the best overall combination of wealth capacity, inclination and philanthropic priority.

☐ The chief development officer has enlisted a variety of perspectives in creating and regularly updating the list, ensuring it is the best possible list.

☐ The organization has a regular and rigorous process in place to ensure that the list is kept current and that top leaders know who is on the list.

Shared Objectives

☐ The organization knows the philanthropic objectives of prospective principal gift donors—objectives in general, in addition to those that pertain to the organization specifically.

☐ Prospective principal gift donors have a seat at the table when it comes to the development of organizational objectives, especially long-term, strategic objectives.

☐ Donors are engaged in planning to the degree that some of the largest gifts become largely self-initiated and self-solicited.

Big Ideas

☐ The organization has an inclusive and regular process for generating, vetting and approving big ideas.

☐ The organization has defined clear and compelling objectives that require gifts at least twice the size of the organization's largest gifts to date.

☐ Organizational leaders have and demonstrate confidence that the organization is prepared to accept principal gifts and use them well, making donors proud to engage in philanthropic partnership at the organization's highest levels of giving.

☐ Donors are engaged in developing and providing lead gifts designated toward big ideas.

Relationship Builders

☐ The CEO, board chair, development/campaign chair and chief development officer are fully committed to principal gift fundraising. They have allocated sufficient time and other resources to the effort.

☐ A principal gift steering committee, supported by the chief development officer, is in place.

☐ A relationship-building team, and a point person for that team, has been identified for each prospective principal gift donor.

☐ Relationship builders are supported and coordinated—rather than "controlled"—so that they can develop authentic relationships and make their best contributions.

Engagement

☐ A current, customized engagement plan is in place for each prospective principal gift donor, and members of relationship-building teams are aware, as appropriate.

☐ Board leaders are engaged, as appropriate, in considering prospective principal gift donors for board seats and other leadership positions.

☐ In addition to board, advisory board, committee and council membership opportunities, time-limited engagement opportunities are regularly discussed and developed.

☐ Senior leaders know names and current, top-level information about all prospective principal gift donors and keep them top of mind.

☐ The chief development officer keeps senior leaders and their executive assistants informed and up to date on relevant information on prospective principal gift donors.

Ultimate Gifts

☐ A long-term, customized stewardship plan is in place that will survive changes in fundraising personnel.

Appendix D

PRINCIPAL GIFTS POSITION DESCRIPTION—COMPONENTS AND CONSIDERATIONS

These components and considerations will assist in creating position descriptions of principal gift officers, principal gift coordinators and the chief development officer, depending on the size and structure of the organization.

☐ Responsible for building, supporting, and sustaining healthy, productive and mutually beneficial relationships between prospective principal gift donors and the organization. Principal gift donors and prospective donors include those with wealth capacity, inclination toward the organization and likelihood of making the organization a philanthropic priority that, when combined, give them the potential to emerge as a donor of one of the organization's largest gifts.

☐ Ensures that principal gift relationships involve multiple senior organizational leaders. These might include the CEO, board members, senior officers, senior program leaders, other principal gift donors and other staff members including members of the development team.

☐ Supports relationship builders by gathering and sharing information with those involved, coordinating in a supportive but non-obstructive way the interaction between leaders and donors and driving the creation, implementation, regular updating and shared understanding of strategies designed to deepen the relationship between donor and organization.

- ☐ Serves as principal staff person to the organization's principal gift steering committee, or supports the chief development officer in doing so.
- ☐ Plays a front-line role with principal gift donors and prospective donors when such a role is an important component of the overall donor-organization relationship strategy.
- ☐ Ensures that principal gift donors and prospective donors are regularly invited—as appropriate—to make annual fund gifts, make major gifts, make leadership and challenge gifts, support special events, assist in engaging and thanking other donors and otherwise participate in regular philanthropic and volunteer support that deepens the donors' philanthropic partnerships with the organization.

Performance is measured in multiple ways:
- ☐ First and foremost, effectiveness will be measured by the degree to which relationships are broadened and deepened—the number of people involved in each prospective principal gift donor-organization relationship, the number of interactions between these relationship builders and prospective principal gift donors, the number of substantive engagements between donors and organization (gifts, volunteer activities, participation in task forces and other discussions advancing strategic objectives, substantive meetings with senior officers, etc.), the number of gifts made to the annual fund and special events, the number of major/leadership/challenge gifts made and, ultimately, the number of principal gifts made (gifts that are among the largest the organization receives).
- ☐ Performance also will be measured in the quality of support provided to colleagues involved in relationship-building with principal gift donors—the extent to which the person in this role is viewed by senior organizational leaders as an effective strategist, a consensus builder, an effective communicator, a collaborative colleague and a valued thought partner.

Additional note:
- ☐ Major gift officers with existing relationships are sometimes the best people to serve as the primary managers and facilitators of relationships with prospective donors newly designated as prospective principal gift donors. In this case, a principal gifts officer may play a supportive

role, helping the major gifts officer, chief development officer and others track and coordinate efforts across the entire organization and the entire principal gift prospect pool. Or, if the major gift officer has several prospective principal gift donors, the major gift officer might more appropriately sit in on regular principal gift meetings as an adjunct member of the principal gift team.

SUMMARY OF KEY DIFFERENCES BETWEEN MAJOR AND PRINCIPAL GIFT FUNDRAISING

Identification

☐ Prospective *major gift* donors have the capacity and inclination to make large gifts relative to the organization's needs. That combination of capacity and inclination is large enough to warrant management of the donor-organization relationship by an assigned development staff member (a major gift officer, for example).

☐ Prospective *principal gift* donors have the capacity and inclination to make one of the organization's largest gifts. Often, the organization is a focus of their philanthropy.

Engagement

☐ Prospective *major gift* donors have one relationship manager who is responsible for supporting a strong and sustained donor-organization relationship. The relationship manager will likely be directly involved in the relationship and, ideally, will support one or two other relationships between donor and organization. Engagement activities will include those designed for groups—such as gala events, class reunions and special tours—and as many one-on-one meetings and experiences as can be managed (likely only a few per year per prospective donor, on average).

- ☐ Prospective *principal gift* donors have a relationship building team supported by a relationship manager. Ideally, they have many and varied relationships with the organization, coordinated more than controlled by the relationship manager. The relationship manager may or may not be among those interacting regularly with the donor. Though some engagement may happen through activity designed for groups of potential donors, engagement strategies are highly customized and involve much more frequent one-on-one interaction with the donor. Senior organizational leaders keep these donors top of mind.

Solicitation

- ☐ Prospective *major gift* donors will usually be solicited by an organizational representative—such as a development staff member or volunteer/peer donor. Ideally, the gift discussion will flow naturally from discussions about alignment of organizational goals and donor passions and objectives. Organizational representatives endeavor to connect donors with established fundraising objectives and giving opportunities.

- ☐ Prospective *principal gift* donors, once true philanthropic partnership is built, often initiate gift discussions on their own. In many cases, they consider their largest gifts to be self-solicited. The relationship is so strong, and their knowledge is so deep, that an actual request for funds may not be required. In a solicitation discussion, if it does need to occur, the solicitor rarely wonders whether a gift will be made. If there is a question, it is more likely about the size, structure or timing of the gift. Organizational representatives engage donors in strategic planning processes, developing a deeper sense of shared ownership of strategic goals.

Stewardship

- ☐ Stewardship for all donors is critically important. Donors want to be thanked, and most want to be recognized. Even more, they want their gifts to be used wisely, and they want their gifts to make a difference. Gratitude is not enough—organizations owe donors results. While all donors deserve expressions of appreciation and reports on the impact of their giving, it is impractical to provide personalized stewardship for every gift at every level. Stewardship for *major gift* donors should be personalized to the degree possible.

☐ At the very least, assigned *major gift* officers should report on past gifts during their regular visits with donors. In some cases, there will be sufficient resources to support personalized stewardship activity such as a lunch for a donor and the student recipient of the donor's endowed scholarship fund. In other cases, resources may be limited to group activity, such as a pizza party for all student scholarship recipients at which they would be asked to write letters to scholarship donors, or an annual scholarship event to which all recipients and donors would be invited.

☐ Stewardship plans for *principal gift* donors must always be personalized and customized, and they are likely to be complex. They will often include, for example:

  ☐ Family members, or, in the case of foundations and corporations, multiple interested parties. Financial and legal advisors may also be involved.

  ☐ Tracking and appropriately following up on multi-component gift structures—involving lead trusts or remainder trusts, for example, or involving money from a variety of sources such as personal funds and family foundation funds.

  ☐ Many years or even decades of attention—when more than one generation of family members are involved, or when bequests are involved, for example.

  ☐ Engagement of many relationship builders. Some of these may be retired from the position of CEO or from board service but are still important to the donor.

  ☐ Several stewardship officers and excellent communication during handoff. The stewardship officer at the time of the original gift may be long retired or even deceased when the final parts of a gift are received or the final aspects of a project are completed.

REFERENCES

Collins, Chuck, Flannery, Helen, and Hoxie, Josh. 2016. *Gilded Giving: Top Heavy Philanthropy in an Age of Extreme Inequality*. Institute for Policy Studies. http://www.ips-dc.org/wp-content/uploads/2016/11/Gilded-Giving-Final-pdf.pdf.

Di Mento, Maria, and Singh, Nidhi. 2018. "Philanthropy 50: Where They Live, Where They Give, and More." *The Chronicle of Philanthropy*. https://www.philanthropy.com/article/Philanthropy-50-Where-They/242469.

Levis, Bill. 2015. "The 80-20 Rule Is Alive and Well in Fundraising." Association of Fundraising Professionals, Feb. 5. http://afpfep.org/blog/8020-rule-alive-well-fundraising/.

Panas, Jerold. 2005. *Mega Gifts: Who Gives Them, Who Gets Them*. Medfield, MA: Emerson and Church.

Schiller, Ronald J. 2013. *The Chief Development Officer: Beyond Fundraising*. Lanham, MD: Rowman & Littlefield.

Schiller, Ronald J. 2015. *Belief and Confidence: Donors Talk About Successful Philanthropic Partnerships*. Washington: Council for Advancement and Support of Education.

The Chronicle of Philanthropy. 2017. "How America Gives: Breaking the Charity Habit." https://www.philanthropy.com/specialreport/special-report-how-america-gi/154.

U.S. Trust (Bank of America) and IUPUI (Lilly Family School of Philanthropy). 2016. *The 2016 U.S. Trust Study of High Net Worth Philanthropy: Charitable Practices and Preferences of Wealthy Households*. http://www.ustrust.com/publish/content/application/pdf/GWMOL/USTp_ARMCGDN7_oct_2017.pdf.

INDEX

chief development officers (*continued*)
  in identification of donors,
    16–17, 85
  on principal gift steering
    committees, 43, 86
  in relationship building, 38–40,
    42, 48
  roles and responsibilities of,
    16–17, 44–45, 87
chief executive officers (CEOs)
  access to, 50
  confidence in, 4
  engagement with donors, 56–57
  in identification of donors,
    16–17
  on principal gift steering
    committees, 43
  in relationship building, 38–39,
    42, 48
Child, Tim, 84
Chronicle of Philanthropy
  (magazine), 16, 47
Cornell University, 28
culture, organizational. *See*
  organizational culture
customized engagement strategies,
  52–54, 59

D

donors, 9–23. *See also* fundraising;
  gifts
  age of, xviii, 16, 55–56, 78–80
  belief and confidence in
    organizations, 1, 3–6, 29, 35
  criteria for selection of, 9–12, 17
  engagement with. *See*
    engagement with donors

gathering information on,
  12–13, 20
giving capacity of, 14–15, 30, 49
identification of, 2, 7–12, 16–17,
  85, 93
impact of giving on, 82, 84
inclination for giving, xvii, 10,
  12–13, 15, 17, 93
leading by example, 33–34, 41
life cycle of donor relationship,
  19–20
maturation of, 83
number of prospective donors to
  target, 7–8
partnership with. *See*
  philanthropic partnerships
philanthropic priority of,
  9–15, 17
in planning process, 20, 21, 23,
  26–27, 50, 86
recognition of, xx, 77, 94–95
relationships with. *See*
  relationship building
scale of gifts by, 11, 15, 20, 28
self-solicitation by, 5–6, 34–35,
  50, 86
shared objectives with
  organizations, 19–23, 28, 86
timelines of, 21–22
wealth capacity of, xvii, 3, 9–10,
  14, 17
Dunlop, David, 28, 57, 66, 72,
  73, 75

E

80-20 rule, xv, xvi
endowments, 25, 27, 32–33, 74, 76

H

I

K

L

M

N

O

shared objectives with donors,
19–23, 28, 86

P

ACKNOWLEDGMENTS

My first mentor in fundraising, Dave Dunlop, introduced me to principal gifts fundraising and to the joy of philanthropic partnership—for development professionals and for the philanthropists they support.

My colleagues on the faculty of CASE's Inspiring Largest Gifts of a Lifetime conference—Kevin Heaney, Kathleen Loehr, Robert Sharpe, Rebecca Smith, and David Voss—have added immeasurably to my knowledge of successful approaches to principal gifts and to my satisfaction in a career in fundraising. Rebecca, a colleague and friend of several decades, and the chair of the Inspiring Largest Gifts conference, contributed the foreword. Robert contributed an essay on ultimate giving and the baby boom that is included as Appendix A.

Contributors to the words of wisdom about a joyful career in philanthropy include: Tim Child, Walt Dryfoos, David Dunlop, Susan Feagin, Jon Kevin Gossett, Trish Jackson, Robbee Kosak, Mark Kostegan, Michael Leto, Susan Paresky, Jaime Porter, Shelley Semmler, Greg Sheridan, Curt Simic, Rebecca Smith, Gene Tempel, Jim Thompson and Tom Tseng.

I am grateful for the encouragement, insights, and critical feedback of many readers, including Tim Child, senior consultant, Aspen Leadership Group, and former director of principal gifts at the University of Chicago; Alan Fletcher, president and CEO, Aspen Music Festival and School; James Gandre, president, Manhattan School of Music; Don Hasseltine, senior consultant, Aspen Leadership Group, and former vice president for development, Brown University; Kevin Heaney, vice president for advancement, Princeton University; Robert Hurst, philanthropist, chairman of the executive committee of the Whitney Museum of American Art, and chairman of the board of the Aspen Music Festival and School; Gregory Leet, vice president for advancement, The Jackson Laboratory; Kathleen Loehr, principal, Kathleen Loehr & Associates, and former senior vice president for development, American Red Cross; Robin Merle, former senior vice president and chief development officer, Hospital for Special Surgery; Scott Mory, vice president for university advancement, Carnegie Mellon University; Laura Simic, vice president for university advancement, Boise State University; Rebecca Smith, vice president for development, University of Hawaii Foundation; Robert Steel, philanthropist, former chairman of the board of the Aspen Institute and former chairman of the board of Duke University; and Michael Vann, vice president for search management, Aspen Leadership Group.

Doug Goldenberg-Hart, director of editorial projects at CASE at the time this book was launched, has been a friend from the day we met. I'm grateful for his encouragement and wisdom. My thanks also to staff from CASE, including Stephen Pelletier, Jennifer Anderson, and Kris Apodaca, who shepherded the book through the final stages of publication with great care.

Unwavering support for this book came, as it comes each day in every aspect of my life, from my husband, Alan Fletcher, who is himself a brilliant principal gift fundraiser.

I am grateful to the hundreds of philanthropic individuals and families and representatives of corporate and foundation funders who have taught me more than anyone about what works—and what does not work—in fundraising, including and especially lessons about how to build and sustain philanthropic partnerships that transform both organizations and the generous donors who make those organizations a principal beneficiary of their generosity. This book is dedicated to them.

ABOUT THE AUTHOR

Ron Schiller began his development career in the late 1980s at his alma mater, Cornell University, one of the largest and most mature development programs at the time. During those years, the university undertook higher education's first-ever campaign over $1 billion. In the past 30 years, Ron has played an administrative or volunteer leadership role in nine fundraising campaigns with goals ranging from $1.5 million to $4.5 billion.

One of Ron's mentors at Cornell was Dave Dunlop. Dave created Cornell's principal gifts program, one of the first of its kind in the country. Dave also co-created a conference for CASE called "Inspiring the Largest Gifts of a Lifetime." In 2007, Dave invited Ron to join the faculty of that conference, and Ron has been on the faculty ever since.

Ron played a leadership role in creating principal gift programs at Carnegie Mellon University, where he served as Campaign Director, and at the University of Chicago, where as Vice President he led a team of more than 450 staff members that completed a $2.38 billion campaign and secured the university's first two nine-figure gifts ($100 million and $300 million).

Ron then served as President of the National Public Radio Foundation. In the first year of a principal gift program established by Ron and his colleagues, NPR had as many seven-figure-gift donors as it had had in all 40 previous years combined.

Ron has served on many boards, including the Cornell University Council, the Harris Theater for Music and Dance Board of Trustees, the Board of Trustees of the North Carolina School of the Arts, the American Academy in Rome Development Committee and the boards of directors of the American Friends of Covent Garden, the Buddy Program of Aspen, the Cayuga

Chamber Orchestra, the Mendelssohn Choir of Pittsburgh and the Salt Bay Chamberfest. He is currently President of the Alumni Board of the Cornell University Glee Club.

Ron serves as Founding Partner of the Aspen Leadership Group and the Philanthropy Career Network. He interacts daily with nonprofit leaders and philanthropists and contributes regularly to journals in the field of philanthropy. His first book, *The Chief Development Officer: Beyond Fundraising*, was published by Rowman & Littlefield in 2013; his second book, *Belief and Confidence: Donors Talk About Successful Philanthropic Partnership*, was published by CASE Books in 2015. In addition to serving on the faculty of the annual CASE conference, "Inspiring the Largest Gifts of a Lifetime," he has served multiple times as co-chair of CASE's Winter Institute for Chief Development Officers. He is a regular speaker for regional and national conferences of the Association of Fundraising Professionals, the Association for Healthcare Philanthropy and Rice University's Center for Philanthropy and Nonprofit Leadership, among others.

ABOUT CASE

The **Council for Advancement and Support of Education (CASE)** is the professional organization for advancement professionals at all levels who work in alumni relations, communications and marketing, development and advancement services.

CASE's membership includes nearly 3,700 colleges, universities, and independent elementary and secondary schools in more than 80 countries. This makes CASE one of the largest nonprofit education associations in the world in terms of institutional membership. CASE serves more than 88,000 advancement professionals on the staffs of member institutions.

CASE has offices in Washington, D.C., London, Singapore and Mexico City. The association produces high-quality and timely content, publications, conferences, institutes and workshops that assist advancement professionals in performing more effectively and serving their institutions.